Writing Business and Personal Letters

CONTENTS

Introduction

PART 1 – THE IMPORTANCE OF LANGUAGE.

PART TWO WRITING LETTERS

6. Writing business letters

Introduction

This book is a brief introduction to the art of letter writing. After long deliberation, I decided not to produce a book full of standard letters for the reader to copy rote fashion. Although many books of this nature do exist, there seems no point in merely allowing the reader to copy someone else's work.

The main point when producing letters is that the writer must understand the very essence of the language in which he or she is writing. This involves understanding grammar and punctuation – in short understanding the basis of the language, in this case the English language.

Mastery of language and the ability to express oneself, in the business or personal domains, is a wonderful achievement. Mastery and effective use of language is akin to painting a beautiful picture.

This book dwells at the outset on grammar and punctuation and other finer points of the language. It shows the writer of the business or personal letter how to express what it is they are trying to say, how to lay it out and how to take care that the letter achieves its aim.

This little book is rigorous but rewarding. It does not seek to layout 50 different types of letter but to show the reader how to understand the complexities of the language and to coach the reader into a position where he or she will begin to enjoy the language more and to produce an effective letter, whether of a personal or business nature.

****

PART 1.

THE IMPORTANCE OF LANGUAGE

1

The Importance of Punctuation

There are a number of essential elements key to effective letter writing, whether business or personal letters. Basic punctuation is extremely important.

Consider how you speak to someone. Generally, what you say is not one long breathless statement. It is punctuated by full stops. When writing, think about how you would verbalise the same statement and insert full stops as appropriate. For example:

We went walking today and we stopped at a shop and bought something to eat and sat down and ate the food and then decided to move on we walked as far as we could before deciding to sit down and take a rest after half an hour we then decided to turn back-------

Immediately, it is obvious that this statement is one long sentence which would leave the listener, or in turn the reader, confused. The correct version might be:

We went walking today, and we stopped at a shop and bought something to eat. We sat down and ate the food and then decided to walk on. We walked as far as we could before deciding to sit down and take a rest. After half an hour we decide to turn back-

The main point is that by inserting full stops we add structure to a sentence.

The use of commas

Whilst full stops are very important in order to add structure and also to separate out one sentence from the next, sometimes there can be a tendency to use commas instead of full stops. Commas have a particular role but can never take the place of full stops.

Commas are used to add a pause to a statement before concluding with a full stop. They are also used to separate items in a list. When using commas to separate items in a list the last one must be preceded by `and'.

For example:

Dave liked swimming, football, ice hockey, mountain climbing, fell walking *and* judo.

Another example:

Peter was preparing his homework for the next day, his mother was cooking, his father was reading the paper *and* his sister was listening to music.

Beginning a sentence with a conjunction (joining word)

If you begin a sentence with a conjunction (joining word,) put a comma to separate the first part of the sentence from the rest of it. In this sentence, 'if' is a joining word and there is a comma after 'word'.

Here are two more examples with the conjunction underlined. Notice where the comma is placed:

Because it was snowing, we decided to stay inside.
As the sun set, the sky glowed.

Commas are used to separate groups of words within a sentence, in order to give statements within sentences more emphasis. Commas are used in many other areas too, such as before a question (I am not sure about that, are you?) or before a name (do be silent, Jack).

The most important element here, as with full stops, is that when you are composing a letter, think about what you are saying, to whom you are addressing it, and take time to punctuate the statement. This means that the person reading the letter can immediately relate to the contents and can interpret the message.

Making use of semi-colons, colons and the dash

The semi-colon is a very useful punctuation mark. It can be used when you feel that you do not need a full stop; usually the second statement follows closely to the first one. A capital letter is not used after a semi-colon. For example:

The road was getting busier; it was obvious that the traffic was starting to build up.

The idea of traffic building up follows on naturally from the road getting busier. In this case, it might be tempting to use a comma. However, as both statements follow on so closely a semi-colon is more appropriate.

The colon

A colon can be used for two purposes. It can introduce a list of statements, as in the following example:

There are two reasons why you failed: you lost your way, it was dark and you did not follow my orders.

Like the semi-colon you need no capital letter after the colon. The colon can also be used to show two statements reinforcing each other:

Your general punctuation is weak: you must learn to use the full stop and comma more effectively.

Using the dash

A dash is used for emphasis. What is said between dashes – or after the dash if there is only one – is more emphatic than if there were no dash. If you break your sentence in the middle to make an added point, use a dash before and after it:

Peter, Dave, Fred Grace – in fact everyone – had decided to go.

Use of the question mark

We have considered full stops, commas, semi-colons, colons and the use of the dash. We now need to consider the question mark.

The question mark is obviously placed at the end of the question. You should always remember to include the question mark as, if it is missed, the reader of a letter might not take your question to be a question, but a statement.

Example

Is it raining outside?

You are not intending to go out in this weather, are you?

The second question is clearly a mixture of statement and question. To be understood as a question it is important to insert a question mark at the end. If you are using direct speech, the question mark takes the place of the comma and is always placed inside the inverted commas (speech marks):

'When are you going?' asked Susan.

Use of exclamation marks

The exclamation mark should be used rarely otherwise it loses its impact. It should not be used for emphasis; your choice of words should be sufficient to provide the necessary emphasis. It is used in direct speech, again in place of a comma. There should always be an exclamation mark if the word 'exclaimed' is used: 'I cannot believe you said that! She exclaimed.

Putting punctuation into practice.

Having discussed very basic punctuation, the main elements of which you will always use in letters, it is time to do a basic exercise.

Punctuate the following:

1. Dave was very angry with the garage he had bought the car from them and they had stated that the car was in perfect condition at least they had said that he would have no problem with it the car had been nothing but a problem and now he had lost his rag and decided to confront the owner and try to get his money or some of it back.

2. I don't think that is true she exclaimed

What don't you think is true he said?

It cannot be true that every time I go out I see the same person following me he seems to know my exact movements and I am very worried now.

3. I feel that I am knocking my head against a brick wall I have asked my mother father brother and sister what they think of my painting I felt that I had to ask them all by the way and all of them ignored me its as if I have offended them or something or they are to embarrassed to comment.

Now read the key points from Chapter 1.

Key points from Chapter 1

- Basic punctuation is one of the most important elements of effective letter writing.

- By inserting elements of punctuation we add structure to our letter.

- Whilst full stops are used to add structure, commas are used to add a pause and emphasis to a statement.

- Make effective use of colons, semi-colons and dashes.

- Question marks and exclamation marks must only be used when asking a question or adding emphasis.

2

The Importance of Grammar

Making use of your sentence

Using nouns correctly

Nouns are a list of 'things'. The following are typical nouns: car, clock, computer, mechanic, spanners, and so on.

Each of the above words can be the subject of a sentence if it is linked to a verb:

The garage *was* closed

The mechanic *arrived* late

The clock *fell* off the wall

The noun is the subject of the sentence and the verb, which is italicised in the above brief statements, is the doing word. A noun must be linked to a verb if it is to make sense.

Using verbs correctly

A verb is a 'doing' or 'being' word. There must be at least one verb in a sentence otherwise it is not a sentence.

Understanding verbs

Verbs can be either finite or non-finite.

Finite verbs

Finite verbs must show tense. They can be past, present or future and are always connected to a noun or pronoun. (more about pronouns later.)

Consider the verbs and tenses in the following statements:

Tomorrow I will travel to Bristol

Yesterday she was unhappy

He plays the guitar extremely well

'will travel' is the future tense.

'was' is the past tense.

'plays' is the present tense.

Non-finite verbs

The non-finite verbs are the infinitive form of the verb and the present and past participles.

The infinitive

The infinitive is the form of verb that has 'to' before it:

To run, to sing, to eat, to walk.

Many people consider it incorrect to use a 'split infinitive'. This is when a word is placed between the 'to' and the verb:

It is difficult *to* accurately *assess* the data
The following example is better. The infinitive 'to assess' has not been 'split' by the adverb 'accurately'

It is difficult accurately *to assess* the data.

Past participles

The past participle is used with the verb 'to have'; it then forms a finite verb. Either the present or the past tense of the verb 'to have' can be used. It will depend on the context. Look at the following examples. The past participles are italicised:

She had *scratched* her leg.

He has *passed* his driving test.

David has *prepared* supper.

Peter had *written* a letter to his father.

The first three participles in the examples above are the same as the ordinary past tense but 'has' or 'had' have been added. In the last example the past participle 'written' is different and can only be used with the verb 'to have'.

Present participle

The present participle always ends in '-ing' and is introduced by the verb 'to be'. The past or present tense of the verb 'to be' can be used:

David is *helping* his mother.

Susan was *washing* the car.

Using the gerund

The present principle can also be used as a noun. In this case it is called a gerund:

Shopping is fun.

The *wailing* was continuous.

Using the present participle as an adjective
Certain present participles can also be used as adjectives:

The *crying* child ran to its mother.

The *howling* dog kept the family awake.

Now look at the following examples:

Rushed across the road.
Came into the shop.

Are these sentences? Of course they are not. Although they each have a verb, they have no subject linked to them. We don't know who rushed across the road or came into the shop. Add a noun and it makes sense:

The dog rushed across the road

The woman came into the shop.

In each sentence there must be a noun which is linked to a verb.

The above represents basic grammar, which, if linked with correct punctuation, helps you to structure a coherent and understandable letter that will be readily understood and will also instil a certain respect in the reader. If you require a more intense introduction to grammar there are a number of useful books on the market. Many colleges also run courses.

Paragraphing letters

Look at the following example:

John was very used to intimidating others. Every Saturday he would go into the local pub, sit there patiently until his friends started to drift in, and then begin hectoring them and generally 'winding them up'. Johns friends were very used to this and they put up with it because they knew him of old and, in many cases, gave as good as they got. One day, however, John sat as usual in the pub and he noticed that none of his friends had appeared, as was the norm. Another hour passed and still they had not showed up. John phoned Dave on his mobile. Dave answered and he stated that he was fed up with Johns hectoring, as were his friends. John wondered what to do in the face of the rejection of his friends. He was worried and it caused him to reflect on his behaviour. He came to the conclusion that he should visit them and discuss the problem.

The above is one long sentence, which should be broken into paragraphs. Paragraphs can vary into length but each paragraph deals with one topic. The positioning of the topic sentence can vary. The following example shows the above in paragraph form:

John was very used to intimidating others. Every Saturday he would go into the local pub, sit there patiently until his friends started to drift in, and then begin hectoring them and generally 'winding them up'. Johns friends were very used to this and they put up with it because they knew him of old and, in many cases, gave as good as they got.

One day, however, John sat as usual in the pub and he noticed that none of his friends had appeared, as was the norm. Another hour passed and still they had not showed up. John phoned Dave on his mobile. Dave answered and he stated that he was fed up with Johns hectoring, as were his friends. John wondered what to do in the face of the rejection of his friends. He was worried and it caused him to reflect on his behaviour. He came to the conclusion that he should visit them and discuss the problem.

Using quotation marks

Inverted commas are also used to enclose quotations and titles:
She went to the cinema to see the film 'Star wars'.
'A stitch in time saves nine' is a famous proverb.

The expression 'of the minds eye' comes from Shakespeare's play 'Hamlet'.

Notice that the full stop has been placed outside the inverted commas when the quotation or title is at the end of the sentence.

Now read the key points from Chapter 2, Grammar.

****

Key points from Chapter 2

- Nouns are a list of things, a verb is a doing word.

- There must be at least one verb in a sentence otherwise it is not a sentence.

- Verbs can be either finite or non-finite.

- The past participle is used with the verb 'to have'.

- The present participle always ends in '-ing' and is introduced by the verb 'to be'.

- By paragraphing letters you break down the flow of writing and introduce structure.

3

Spelling

English spelling is not easy to learn. There are, of course, some rules. However, there are exceptions to these rules. Some spelling and pronunciation appear to be illogical. It is therefore very important that certain spellings are learnt.

There are 26 letters in the English alphabet. Five are vowels and the rest are consonants.

Forming words

The vowels are A,E,I,O,U. All words have to contain at least one vowel ('Y' is considered to be a vowel in words like 'rhythm' and 'psychology') Consonants are all the other letters that are not vowels. So that a word can be pronounced easily, vowels are placed between them. No more than three consonants can be placed together. Below are two lists. The first contains some words with three consecutive consonants and the second are words with two consecutive consonants:

(a) school, scream, chronic, Christian, through, splash.

(b) Flap, grab, occasion, commander, baggage, added.

All the words in the examples have the consonants separated by vowels.

Forming plurals

To form a plural word an 's' is usually added to a noun. There are some exceptions. If a noun ends in 'y' and there is a consonant before it, a plural is formed by changing the 'y' into an 'i' and adding '-ies':

Lady = ladies
nappy = nappies
company = companies
berry = berries

If the 'y' is preceded by another vowel, an 's' only is added:

monkey = monkeys
donkey = donkeys
covey = coveys

If a noun ends in 'o' and a consonant precedes the 'o', '-es' is added to form a plural:
potato = potatoes
tomato = tomatoes
hero = heroes

32

If there is a vowel before the 'o' an 's' only is added:

studio = studios
zoo = zoos
patio = patios

Changing the form of a verb

When a verb ends in 'y' and it is necessary to change the tense by adding other letters, the 'y' is changed into an 'i' and 'es' or 'ed' is added:

He will *marry* her tomorrow

He was *married* yesterday

A dog likes to *bury* his bone

A dog always *buries* his bone

Using long vowels and short vowels

There is often a silent 'e' at the end of the word if the vowel is 'long':
Date, bite, hope, late, dupe.

Each of these words consists of one syllable (one unit of sound) if another is added, the 'e' is removed:

Date = dating

Bite = biting

And so on.

Adding '-ly' to adjectives

When forming an adverb from an adjective 'ly' (not ley) is added. If there is a 'y' at the end of the adjective, it must be changed to an 'i':

Adjective	Adverb
Happy	Happily
Beautiful	Beautifully
Quick	Quickly
Slow	Slowly

'I' before 'e' except after 'c'.

This rule seems to have been made to be broken. Some words keep to it but some break it. Here are some that follow the rule. All of them are pronounced 'ee' – as in 'seed':

No 'c' in front	After 'c'
niece	ceiling
piece	receive
grief	deceive

Exceptions to this rule are:

Neighbours, vein, either, neither, seize, weird.

Using a dictionary

Checking your spelling

Use a dictionary frequently to check your spelling. Don't guess the spelling of a word. Look it up. It is helpful to keep a list of words that you have misspelled so that you can learn them.

Looking at words

A dictionary not only tells you how to spell a word. It also tells you what part of speech the word is. Sometimes the word appears more than once as it has different meanings and can be used as a different part of speech. Look at the following examples:

Land (noun)   (a)   The solid part of the earth

(b)   A country

Land (verb)

(c) To go ashore or bring a plane down to the ground

The dictionary will also often give the derivation of a word. English is a rich language that owes much to other languages. If you have time, browse through a dictionary looking at the derivation of some of the words. It can be a fascinating experience.

Making use of the thesaurus

A thesaurus can be very useful. It will help you to find an alternative word (synonym) for a word that you have used too much. Words are shown alphabetically and beside each will be a list of words that could replace the word that you want to lose. Not all synonyms will be suitable. It depends on the context of the word.

Now read the key points from Chapter 3, spelling, overleaf.

****

Key points from Chapter 3

■ There are 26 letters in the English alphabet, 5 are vowels and the rest consonants.

■ Every word has a vowel

■ No more than three consonants can be placed together.

■ Use a dictionary frequently to check your spelling.

■ A thesaurus will provide many alternatives to a word.

4

Apostrophes and Abbreviations

Using apostrophes to show possession

Apostrophes are put at the end of nouns when the nouns have something belonging to them.

Making a singular noun possessive

If a noun is singular and it has something belonging to it, add an apostrophe and an 's'. For singular words that show possession the apostrophe is always placed before the 's':

Karen's handbag was stolen.
Her neighbour's fence was blown down.
The child's ball bounced over the wall.

If the singular noun already ends in an 's' another 's' should still be added:

The princess's bridal gown was made by a well-known couturier.
The thief stole the Duchess's jewels.

However, in some cases, the extra 's' can be omitted as in the following cases:

James' book was missing

He damaged his Achilles' tendon.

Making a plural noun possessive

Most nouns add an 's' to make a plural. In this case the apostrophe goes after the noun if it is possessive:

The thundering of the horses' hoofs broke the silence.
The ladies' gowns were beautiful.

Some nouns do not add an 's' to become a plural. In this case, if they are possessive, they are treated like singular nouns. The apostrophe is added before the extra 's'. Some of these words are: children, men, women, mice, sheep, geese:

The children's playground was vandalised.
Kate watched the mice's tails disappearing round the corner.

Using possessive pronouns correctly

When using the possessive form of a pronoun, apostrophes are not used. The possessive pronouns are: mine, her, his, its, ours, yours and theirs.

The blame is mine (no apostrophe)

These books are hers (no apostrophe)

The first prize was his (no apostrophe)

Abbreviating words

When writing formally, it is better not to abbreviate. Write the words out in full. However, it is, of course, acceptable to abbreviate when writing dialogue.

Using apostrophes to abbreviate words

An abbreviation is when letters are missed out. Sometimes two words are combined into one. An apostrophe is placed where the letter or letters have been omitted:

'Do not' = don't

'Can not' = can't

'Would not' = wouldn't

Note especially that 'Could have' becomes 'could've' not 'could of'. Because of the way the abbreviation in the above example sounds, a common mistake is to use the word 'of' instead of the abbreviation 've'.

Abbreviating words without using apostrophes

When words are shortened, it is usual to put a full stop at the end:

information info.

document   doc.

etcetera   etc.

The names of counties are shortened in the same way and all have full stops after them:

Berkshire Berks.

Nottinghamshire Notts.

Other words that are often abbreviated are titles but some of these should only be abbreviated if the title is followed by the person's full name. A full stop should be put after the abbreviation if it is used:

Capt. Edward Symes

not

Capt. Symes

Handling contractions

Some words are abbreviated by using the first and last letters only. These are contractions of the original word and do not usually need a full stop at the end:

Mister   Mr

Mistress Mrs

Doctor   Dr

No full stop is needed after a contraction.

Using acronyms

It is becoming increasingly common to describe companies or organisations only by the initial letters of the names of the group. This is called an acronym. This is now so prevalent that we often forget what the original letters stood for. It is no longer considered necessary to put a full stop after each capital letter. Here are some reminders of frequently used acronyms:

RADA   Royal Academy of Dramatic Arts

NATO   North Atlantic Treaty Organisation

ASH   Action on Smoking and Health

UNICEF United Nations Children's Fund

RAF   Royal Air Force

And many more!

Now read the key points from Chapter 4, apostrophes and abbreviations.

****

Key points from Chapter 4

■ Apostrophes are put at the end of nouns when the nouns have something belonging to them.

■ If a noun is singular and it has something belonging to it, add an apostrophe and an 's'. For singular words that show possession the apostrophe is always placed before the 's.

■ Most nouns add an 's' to make a plural. In this case the apostrophe goes after the 's' if it is possessive.

■ When writing formally, it is better not to abbreviate.

■ It is becoming more popular to use acronyms to abbreviate companies or organisations.

5

Using the Correct English

Recognising common mistakes

Remember that punctuation is essential if your work is to make sense.

- Do not use commas instead of full stops. If in doubt, put a full stop.
- Remember to put a question mark at the end of a question.

Revising sentence construction

Remember that sentences must make sense. Each sentence must contain at least one subject (noun) and one verb. If there is more than one verb, there are two clauses and these should either be separated by a full stop or a semi-colon or linked by a conjunction.

Revising the correct use of verbs

Always make sure that the nouns and verbs 'agree'. If the noun is singular, the verb should always be singular. Remember that collective nouns are singular and are followed by the singular form of the verb.

The politician is hoping to win tonight.

not

The politician *are* hoping to win tonight.

Avoiding the misuse of pronouns

There is often confusion in the words 'I' and 'me', 'she' and 'her', 'he' and 'him', 'we' and 'us', 'they' and 'them'.

'I', 'she', 'he', 'we', and 'they', are personal pronouns and are usually the subject of the sentence. This means they are the instigators of the action in the sentence:

I like travelling
She went on holiday
He went home
We have no bread
They are going today

'Me, 'her', 'him', 'us', and 'them', are usually the objects of the sentence. This means that something is done to them:

46

The stone hit *me*
The prize was given to *her*
The wall collapsed on *him*
The dog bit *us*
The mother scolded *them*

Revising spelling

- Learn the most commonly misspelled words; for example:

Surprise, disappear, disappoint, independent

- Learn the correct spelling of words that sound the same but are spelt differently; for example:

hear - here
their - there
sea - see
too - two - to

The words 'practice' and 'practise' are often confused and so are 'advice' and 'advise'. 'Practise' and 'advise' are the verbs and 'practice' and 'advice' are the nouns:

You must practise the guitar if you are to improve.
There is a cricket practice at the net today.

I advise you not to do that
Please take my advice.

Other words that are often confused are 'council' and 'counsel', 'compliment' and 'compliment', 'principle' and 'principal' and 'stationery' and 'stationary'.

Avoiding common mistakes

A mistake that is often heard is the following:
He is very different *to* his brother.

This is not correct and should read:

He is very different *from* his brother.

If you **differ,** you move away from. If you are **similar** you are similar to.

Avoiding mistakes when using apostrophes and abbreviations

- Do not put an apostrophe every time there is a plural word ending in 's'.
- The abbreviation of 'could have' is 'could've' not 'could of'.

- Do not put a full stop after a contraction:

Doctor - Dr
Mister - Mr

Avoiding unnecessary repetition

- Remember that nouns do not usually need to be repeated within the same sentence.

-

- Replace them with pronouns

He tried on his new boots. The boots were too tight.

This should be:
He tried on his new boots. *They* were too tight.

Avoiding tautologies

A tautology is where the same thing is said twice over in different ways, for example:

The last chapter will be at the end of the book.
The people applauded by clapping their hands.

These two sentences are repetitious. The meaning is at the beginning of the sentence and has been repeated again at the end. Avoid tautologies.

Varying the sentence

If sentences frequently begin with the same word, the word becomes monotonous. Avoid the temptation to start consecutive sentences in the same way.

She went to the car. She opened the trunk. She closed the trunk. She was upset.

These sentences all start with she so the passage does not flow. It is easy to say the same thing in another way so that it does flow:

Susan went to the car and opened the trunk. Closing the trunk, she was clearly upset.

Making comparisons
When using adjectives to compare two things or people '-er' is usually added to the base word:
big   bigger
tall   taller
slow   slower
happy   happier

When more than two people are involved, '-est' is added to the adjective:

Big   bigger   biggest
Tall   taller   tallest
Slow slower slowest

Some words are so constructed that to add the suffix '-er' or '-est' would produce clumsy words. In this case 'more' and 'most' are put before the adjective instead:

beautiful   more beautiful   most beautiful

intelligent more intelligent   most intelligent

Eliminating jargon

The word 'jargon' derives from a Middle English word meaning 'meaningless chatter'. The derivation suggests a very good reason why jargon should be avoided. Anyone who is a member of a group uses jargon that is intelligible only to other members of the same group.

Lawyers have their own jargon and so do politicians, schoolteachers and nurses. You should use words and expressions that can be easily understood by all and not forms of language that have grown up around professions, for example, as these can often serve to confuse unless you are part of that group.

An example of such words can be words that end in 'ise'. Privatise, normalise, prioritise and so on. Make sure that you use language which is not restricted and is in common use.

Avoiding clichés

Clichés are phrases that are heard over and over again. We all use them and they are often very apt.

Creating similes

'White as a sheet' and 'ran like the wind' are similes. These are comparisons between two things using the words 'like' or 'as'. Many clichés are similes and they are often very vivid. However, they are not original and you should avoid them.

Using metaphors

Metaphors are also comparisons but they are 'implied' and do not use 'like' or 'as'. We use metaphorical language a great deal in everyday speech. It is language that is not literally true but cannot be classified as a lie as everyone knows what is meant.

Look at the following examples:

I'm starving.

He says he's freezing

She's dying of thirst.

All are clichés and all are metaphors. The language is metaphorical – not literally true. If it were true, all three characters would be dead and we know that is not what is meant.

Improving your style
Economising on words

Good writing is simple and easy to understand. Unnecessary words should be eliminated. If one word can replace four then use it.

Using the active voice

The active voice is more positive than the passive voice. In the active voice a subject does something. In the passive voice something is done to him.

Active voice

The father struck his son

The teacher gave his class a detention

Passive voice

The son was struck by his father

The class was given a detention by the teacher

Avoiding negatives

Using positive statements instead of negative ones also economises on words. For example:

He did not remember his wife's birthday.

Clare was not present in the afternoon.

Would be better as the following:

He forgot his wife's birthday

Clare was absent in the afternoon.

Avoid double negatives which make a positive:

There isn't no one there

I haven't got no lunch

The word 'not' and 'no' cancel each other out and therefore the first example means that there is someone there and the second means that I have got lunch.

There is a choice of two correct versions. Only one negative should be used if the sense is to be kept:

There isn't anyone there.

Or

There is no one there.

I haven't got any lunch.

or

I have no lunch.

Developing your own style

By now you should have a good grasp of the basics of English and you should aim to develop your own style of writing. Avoid repetition and vary your sentences. Look at a cross section of other people's styles and begin to develop a style of your own. The art of writing is a very satisfying art, particularly when done with care and attention.

Now read the key points from Chapter 5 overleaf.

****

Key points from Chapter 5.

■ Do not use commas instead of full stops. If in doubt put a full stop.

■ Each sentence must contain at least one noun and one verb.

■ Avoid the misuse of pronouns.

■ Learn the most commonly misspelled words.

■ Avoid common mistakes.

■ Avoid unnecessary repetition.

■ Avoid tautologies.

■ Try to vary sentences.

■ Eliminate jargon and avoid clichés.

■ Economise on words.

■ Develop your own style.

PART 2

WRITING LETTERS

6

Writing Business Letters

Having studied the basics of English grammar, it is now time to construct an effective letter.

Aiming your letter

Letters project images of you and your organisation to the broad outside world. Clients and general customers of your business will build up a picture of you and your organisation from the style of letter that you write.

When you write a letter you should consider to whom you are addressing it. What is the aim of your letter? A clear aim will tell the reader what he or she wishes to know, but also helps you as a writer by telling you what you do not need to write.

A letter provides a permanent record of transactions between organisations. That record will guide future actions and may also appear as evidence in cases where contractual problems are arising and court action is necessary. Your record must be clear and correct.

Ask why you are writing and then you can focus on what your letter is aiming to achieve:

- payment of an overdue account
- sales of a new product
- technical information
- confirmation of a meeting

Who is your reader?

You should give thought to the person who will read your letter. For incoming letters seek guidance from:

- the name of the job or department title at the end
- the content of the letter

If you are initiating correspondence, make sure that you have targeted your reader accurately. It might be worth making a telephone call to ask who deals with a certain area. Once you have done this you can direct your request to the most appropriate person. Buyer and salesman have a different outlook on a similar product. In making a technical enquiry to the buyer you will expect a competent reply: the salesman's competence may direct you to the benefit of buying the product.

One very important point is that the level of your writing must be your natural way of expressing your meaning. If you try to adopt any other style than the one that is natural to you, you will emerge as strained and unnatural.

What does your reader need?

When you respond to a letter, take a close look at what it requires:
- Is it looking for information?
- Does it need action?
- What action does it require and by when?

Consider how to approach the task

Writing acts as a window through which the reader may see the personality that lies behind the words. In certain cases, this can be a disadvantage, for example if you have an indifferent attitude or if other factors have influenced your mood. This will be reflected in the letter. You have to remember that when people read letters they will pick up varied messages, depending on their own personality and your mood and style when writing the letter.

There are advantages. Once that you are aware that your attitude shows in your writing then you can use this to considerable effect. Do not try to hide your personality, let the reader see that you are able to understand the readers problems, that you are willing to help or that you are patient if a mistake has been made or incomplete information has been given.

Your approach will obviously vary considerably depending on who you are writing to. If you are writing to complain about poor service you will expect to be firm in your tone. You are likely to be plain speaking, specifying what is wrong and laying out timescales for action.

If you are writing in reply to a complaint from a customer, a firm approach will be inappropriate. You will need to adopt a different, more conciliatory approach.

In professional firms, letters rarely go beyond the conventional picture of three short paragraphs. These letters may be:

- offering advice of some sort, such as financial advice
- specifying an architects detailed requirements for progress on a job

In handling more extended material you will need a more complete and visible classification of the content. This will show in headings, and perhaps sub-headings within the narrative, to give the required direction to the reader.

Decide where and when to write

The place and timing of your letter is critical. The reader will not be very happy if your letter arrives on the morning that a crucial decision has to be made, a decision which will be influenced by your letter. Neither will that person be happy if the letter goes to the wrong address. This can easily happen where businesses are organised around different addresses. Your sales letter must arrive at the time that relates to the budget, or the buying decision. At the same time it must be persuasive enough to encourage the reader to put it on record in anticipation of such a time.

Now read the key points from Chapter Six, Writing Business Letters.

****

Key points from Chapter Six

■ Letters project images of you and the organisation to the outside world.

■ When you write a letter, you should consider to whom you are addressing it.

■ A letter provides a permanent record of transactions between organisations.

■ Decide when and where to write a letter.

****

7

Planning and Structuring a Letter

Many people who write letters do so in a hurry and will not give a great amount of time or thought to the contents. In some cases, this may be suitable, especially if you are writing a very short letter of acknowledgement. However, in longer business letters that require more elaboration, then this is not appropriate and a great deal more thought needs to be exercised.

A relatively small amount of time is needed to plan and write letters and, in the long run, will save you time and effort. A well-planned letter will ensure that you communicate the right amount of information and detail to the reader.

Many writers sometimes have problems with the opening sentence of a letter. There is the idea that the opening sentence is of the utmost importance and that the rest will flow easily. This is not always the case. When planning a letter, work from the general to the particular. The detail will then tend to fall naturally into place.

The contents of your letter

When determining the content of your letter, you should ask yourself:

- who is my reader?
- What does that person need to know?

If that person needs to know very little, for example that you intend to be at a meeting, a few words will suffice. However, if the person wishes to know quite a lot then you will need to be very methodical in planning the contents of the letter. When approaching such a task:

- gather relevant information
- allocate the information to main sections
- give each main section a heading

With classification it is tempting to choose general or abstract headings that allow the detail to fit comfortably. You will achieve a better result by choosing more selective, more concrete headings.

Decide the sequence of delivery

It is difficult to think about the content of your letter without giving thought to the sequence in which you will deliver it. A natural order will quite often emerge.

When you are resolving a problem:

- what has gone wrong
- why it went wrong
- what will we do to put it right

When you review activity:
- what we have done in the past
- how we operate currently
- what we plan for the future

A natural order promotes a logical flow of thinking and allows the letter to end at the point you wish to reach:

- looking ahead rather than looking back
- solving a problem rather than raising one

For more complicated letters people tend to group their material functionally but find the sequence more challenging and often repeat material. To plan your sequence:

- spread your headings across the top of a sheet of A4 using the landscape or horizontal plane.
- List the points that relate to each heading in columns
- Consider any changes in the sequence

- Decide whether larger sections should break down into sub-headings or whether additional headings would be better.

An outline classification can show your intended approach to a colleague or other. Changes are easy to make and the outline classification will serve as an excellent prompt for your draft letter.

Forming paragraph structure

We discussed paragraph structures earlier on. There are no rules for paragraphing that require text to be broken after a certain number of words or line. Paragraphs have a lot more to do with consistency of thought than length. However, there are guidelines that help to convert planned content into readable paragraphs:

- change paragraph with each change of subject
- if your subject requires lengthy exploration, break it into further paragraphs that reflect the different aspects.
- Headline your paragraph to give an early indication of your subject.

Many business letters are brief and to the point and can be delivered in a single paragraph. The key is to ensure that the reader can follow your train of thought and that your letter is not one long rambling monologue.

Many single page business letters appear in a three-paragraph format that reflects:

- identification
- explanation
- action

In these cases the opening and closing paragraphs are often short – commonly a single sentence. The middle paragraph expands to the extent that it is necessary to complete.

Paragraph length is also about a particular writing style. A single sentence can make an emphatic paragraph but over-use of single sentence paragraphs will diminish their effect.

Control your sentence length

Writers struggling to construct a sentence are usually concerned with finding the right words to convey their intended meaning to the reader. You should avoid the long lead-in to a sentence. Your lead-in should be snappy and direct as opposed to long winded. If you find it difficult to express your thoughts you should think to yourself, what exactly am I trying to say?

Researchers have measured writing to see what makes it readable. Answers usually include the types of words used and the sentence length. The ideal sentence length is usually about twenty words. After this a sentence can tend to become unwieldy.

Words are not just counted between full stops: the colon and semi-colon also determine the sentence structure for this purpose.

You should remember that you are seeking a readable average sentence length: you are not trying to make every sentence twenty words long. Variety in sentence length will produce a more interesting style. You should adopt a conversational approach in your writing, controlling your sentence length.

Use a range of punctuation

Again, in chapter 2, we looked at punctuation generally. Relating this directly to letter writing, the trend is to use only the punctuation you need to reveal your meaning.

The full stop

A sentence must contain a subject and a finite verb; a finite verb is a verb that has been modified by its subject.

A sentence must express a complete thought but can have a very simple structure:

David writes
It is snowing

Semicolon

The semicolon provides a useful pause, lighter than the full stop but heavier than a comma. You will use it most reliably by ensuring that the elements you have linked could appear as independent sentences.

Colon

Many writers in business use the colon to introduce a list:

During the recent visit to the exhibition, the following items were lost: one briefcase, one wallet, one umbrella and a set of keys.

The colon also allows you to define or illustrate an initial statement:

Following my operation, my personal circumstances changed somewhat: I found myself short of money and unable to work.

Commas

There are many technical reasons for using commas but these are mainly to do with building a pause to indicate your meaning on first reading.

- use a comma when you wish to indicate such a pause
- do not break a sentence, unnecessarily with a comma
- Do not use a comma if you need a heavier stop, this section applies even if the next point is linked. (a semi-colon should replace the comma here).

Brackets

Brackets enclose an aside or illustration and need no further punctuation.

There are 5280 feet (or 1760 yards) in a mile

It is useful for husband and wife (in certain circumstances) to hold a joint bank account.

Question marks

Use question marks only for direct questions.

Where are you going?

When are you going to send the cheque?

Now read the key points from Chapter Seven overleaf

****

Key points from Chapter Seven

- Business letters cannot, usually, be written in a hurry. This is especially the case if they are longer letters trying to convey complex information.

- When planning a letter, work from the general to the particular.

- When determining the contents of a letter, you should ask who is your reader and what do they need to know.

- Decide the sequence of delivery.

- Structure your letter.

- Control your sentence length.

- Use a range of punctuation.

8

Layout of Letters

Letters always have a certain convention that distinguishes them from e-mail and memorandum. Letters always begin 'Dear...........' and end 'Yours sincerely.........'. This is the same whatever the nature and tone of the letter, whether you are writing a strong letter of complaint or a more measured letter.

However, letters have become less formal and word processing now gives many more options for the alignment and appearance of text than a layout that was once dictated by the limitations of a typewriter.

The majority of letters are left aligned only, leaving a ragged right margin that appears less formal and aids reading. Key information such as the reference, date, address, salutation, complimentary close and enclosures is increasingly aligned to the left margin.

Letterheads have changed too. Once all information appeared at the top of the page. Now you may see the company logo prominent at the top but much of the statutory detail at the foot.

Quote references in full

We put a reference on a letter so that when someone replies quoting the reference, we are easily able to find the letter on file. Always quote a reference when replying. Much correspondence is stored electronically and the quoted reference may be the only manageable way of retrieving a particular letter.

One common layout will begin:

Reference
Date
Address of reader
....
....

An alternative layout will show:

Address of reader   Your ref:
                                     Our ref:
....   Date:
....
....

In the second example, the information will often appear in print on the company letterhead and the position will reflect the letter template on the word processor.

You should look at the address not simply to direct your letter to the receiving organisation but to the individual from whom you seek a response. It is now usual practice to include the name and job title of the recipient as part of the address. As that information appears through the window of the envelope your information can be targeted unopened to the reader.

Choose an appropriate salutation

Try to include the name in the salutation at the start of your letter. This will:

- get commitment from a reader whom you have targeted precisely
- set a personal tone for your writing

Writers sometimes identify themselves with just name and initials at the end of a letter. However, there is a practical problem in that we need to attach a style (Mr Mrs Miss Ms) to the reply.

Very formal style still appears in business letters. You may find a letter that begins:

(See overleaf)

For the attention of Mrs D Smith

Dear Sirs

We acknowledge receipt of your recent letter...............

A name allows you to be more natural and direct:

Dear Mrs Smith

Thank you for...........

You will need a formal salutation when you write to an institution rather than a named reader.

A PLC or a limited company is a single legal entity and it is logical to address the company as Dear Sir. Avoid writing Dear Sir/Madam. Whichever part of that generalisation applies to it, it is offensive for its failure to relate properly to you. A general name can make a good alternative.

Use informative headings

Most letters will benefit from a heading. This serves to:

-     tell the reader what you are writing about

- provides a descriptive reminder of the content of a letter you may later wish to retrieve.

In an extensive letter distinguish between a heading that covers the broad scope of the letter at the start:

Pullfir Contracts

Annual check J.Peters

Training programme

And the more specific headings that occur at intervals to identify the specific topics of the letter.

In a short letter you may write predominantly on one topic but then wish to make a small unrelated point later. This need produces clichés like:

May I take this opportunity to remind............

While you are right to take the opportunity you will make a clear case by putting your thought under a separate heading. The letter will take on the following form:

Salutation

Heading one

....

....

....

Heading Two

....

Close

Think about the sequence in which you handle your headings. Where possible end with the topic that needs action.

Bullet points form a practical sub-structure for letters. They are best for items that require separate identification but which need no specific reference.

Before we can authorise a mortgage we will require:

- three payslips
- your P60
- proof of residence.

A sub-structure of numbers is helpful where you wish to raise a number of points which require a specific answer from your reader.

Start with the reasons for writing

Use the start of your letter to identify the reason for writing in the first place. When you initiate correspondence, spell out your intention for the reader. A heading will provide the initial view but your opening sequence will sharpen the focus:

- I am writing for information about the catering facilities that you offer.
- I plan to visit Sweden in the Summer

When responding to a letter you have a similar need to provide a clear focus for the reader. You may wish to use the heading from the original letter before responding more specifically:

- Thank you for your letter of 12th July.
- I confirm that our latest range of books will be ideal for your school.
- The plan enclosed with this letter should enable us to progress the matter.

Some very short letters end where they begin:

- Please send me a copy of your latest book and a catalogue
- I can confirm that I will be at the finance meeting next week

End by pointing the way ahead

The end of your letter is important in triggering the action you seek from the reader:

- Please let me know when you will send me my cheque.
- Please send me the completed form with payment by July 16th.

The true aim of the letter may vary from the issue that has prompted it. In such cases project your purpose at the end.

Long letters containing a number of action points may benefit from a short summary of actions at the end. Avoid clichés at the end of your letter. These usually appear when you have covered the ground and are ready to sign off. Padding at this point pushes the required action further back into the letter, making it less of a prompt for the reader's attention.

Matching the end of the letter to the salutation

There is a firm convention for matching the ending of a letter to the opening. If you begin with a proper noun:

Dear Mr Smith
Dear Miss Jones
You end:

Yours sincerely (the 's' is always lower case)
Similarly if you begin with a common noun:

Dear Leaseholder
Dear Lord Mayor

You end:

Yours sincerely

For formal salutations:

Dear Sir
Dear Madam

You end:

Yours faithfully
Composing Business letters

Writing effective letters is not just detailing information. The way you compose the letter, the format, is very important indeed. As well as the reader of the letter, you will need to consider:

- the sequence in which you deliver your letter
- the tone reflected in your choice of language.

Ask yourself, when putting the letter together:

- how firm should you be?
- should you be apologetic?
- Should you send enclosures?

And so on.

The sequence of a letter allows you to move:

- from where you are now
- by means of any supporting information
- to where you want to be.

Choosing an appropriate tone

When you write, your language conveys the content of the letter and the manner of its delivery. You should think very carefully about the words you use and the way you use them. Obviously, each letter is different and, in the context of business, there are many situations that you will need to address, from taking action against a member of staff, against a supplier, to praising someone for good work to chasing late payments.

One strand linking all letters is that of getting to the point as quickly as possible whilst getting the message across. The use of language is an art and a skill and it is very necessary to ensure that you have said all that you have to say, in a clear and (often) sensitive fashion. The aim is to get your message across and to convince or persuade the other of your case.

Summary and sample business letters.

In the last three chapters, several key points have been stressed. Before laying out sample business letters it is important to summarise these points:

- Aim your letter carefully. You should ask yourself why you are writing and who is your intended recipient. What does your reader need?

- Make sure you plan and structure your letter and decide the sequence of delivery. Take pains to ensure that your punctuation is correct and also control your sentence length.

Sample business letters

Overleaf.

Introducing your firm

PRINTING SERVICES LIMITED

Mr D Davies

Askews Castle Ltd

42 Smiths Drive

Aberdeen

Perthshire

Scotland

321

38 King Road

London E17 4PT

Tel: 020 8123 5467

Our ref:

21st July 20

Dear Mr Davies

I am writing to introduce my company to you. We care a business that provides printing services, consultancy and printing machinery to companies in the north of England. Our clients include Nobles, Bloomsbury and Polestar Wheaton Limited. In particular we offer:

- Cost effective printing solutions to meet all requirements.
- Consultancy services. These are designed to ascertain a clients needs.
- Follow up work with recommendations and costing.

At this stage, we enclose our latest brochure for your perusal. If you are interested in our products and services either now or in the future, please call me on my direct line 020 8123 5467. We would be pleased to supply further details on request or to discuss your requirements further.

Yours sincerely

David Askew
Sales manager

**

Offering new products

PRINTING SERVICES LIMITED

Mr D Davies   38 King Road
Askews Castle Ltd   London E17 9PT
42 Smiths Drive
Aberdeen   Tel: 020 8123 5467
Perthshire
Scotland

1st July 201

Dear Mr Davies

We are pleased to introduce the latest addition to our fast expanding range of printing presses, the Digital plus reproduction unit. This innovative product is the latest in a line of presses introduced by Printing Services Limited. It is designed to enable small publishers to cut costs and keep their stock holdings down. There are tow distinctive features that distinguishes our press from others:

- Low print runs of 1 or more can be achieved.
- The press can achieve a two-week turnaround from placing of the order to fulfilment.

For a limited period, we are making a special offer available exclusively to our customers:

A 10% discount off the normal trade price for each press ordered. We enclose sales literature for the press. To take advantage of this offer please ring me direct on 020 8123 5467. Please note that this offer is for a limited period. We look forward to receiving your call.

Yours sincerely

David Askew
Sales Manager

**

Chasing a reluctant buyer

PRINTING SERVICES LIMITED

Mr D Davies

Askews Castle Limited

42 Smith Drive

Aberdeen

Perthshire

Scotland

38 King Road

London E17 9PT

Tel: 020 8123 5467

Ref: 123

24th July 20

Dear Mr Davies

We were delighted to receive your enquiry about our printing press last week. I understand that you expressed interest following a demonstration by our agent. We were sure that you would be impressed with the press and would appreciate the advantages to your company.

We can confirm that this product is still available at a 10% discount to you. However, we have to point out once again that this offer can extend for a limited period only as we have received many expressions of interests and resultant firm sales.

I am pleased to enclose our sales literature for your further perusal and information. Please do not hesitate to contact me to discuss the purchase of our press.

We look forward to hearing from you again.

Yours sincerely
David Askew
Sales manager

The three letters above demonstrate all of the key aims of a business letter. The letter is aimed at the key person, the message is clear. There is a clear understanding of what the reader needs. The letter is planned, structured and the sequence of delivery leaves the reader in no doubt as to the message.

The sentences are short, crisp and to the point. The reader will be very clear about the intent and will be impressed by the layout.

There are many varieties of business letters but the key themes are exactly the same throughout.

Now read the key points from Chapter 8

****

Key points from Chapter 8

- Letters have a certain convention that distinguishes them from e-mail and memoranda.

- Quote any references in full.

- Choose an appropriate salutation.

- Use informative headings.

- Start with the reasons for writing.

- End by pointing the way ahead.

- Choose an appropriate tone.

9

Writing Personal Letters

So far, we have concentrated on the nature and form of business letters. These letters, by their nature, require a great deal of attention to detail as they act primarily as records of business and need to be specific in their aim.

Personal letters, whilst also ideally needing the same level of knowledge of the English language and attention to detail, have a different starting point. This is that they are personal and are often written to people we know and have conversed with many times. Therefore, many elements that we need to be aware of in business letters, such as the avoidance of jargon and clichés, are quite often present in personal letters.

Nevertheless, there are certain formal conventions that need to be observed at the outset.

Personal salutations

The personal letter will differ from the business letter in that you will usually put your name and address on the top right hand side, as with the example overleaf and the date under the address.

The letter will, in many cases, be handwritten, to add to the feeling of intimacy, and will finish not with 'Yours sincerely' but quite often will finish with 'love, or 'regards' or even 'cheers', depending on who you are writing to and how you have written the letter.

See example letter overleaf

Example personal letter.

38 Cromwell Road

Walthamstow

London E17 9JN

3rd May 20

Dear Peter

It was really great to see you at the opening match of the world cup last Wednesday. Hey, what a great game wasn't it? I really loved the first half and, although the second half dragged a bit there was loads of action.

Did you see Stanley Peters? What a real snake in the grass! He was excellent in the first half but was real lazy in the second. He should have been substituted.

Anyway, enough about football. What about you and your family? I hope that you are all faring well and Susan is OK. She is a really nice person and you have a very good partner there.

Well, old buddy, enough said. Once again, it was really great to see you and I look forward to the next time. We should get together a little earlier and maybe have a pint or two, just like old times. We wont overdo it, as we used to, but it would still be a nice break.

I am keeping well. Work is a bit of a bind but there again, isn't all work nowadays. Very stressy. Take care mate, see you soon I hope.

Cheers
Dave

As you can see, this letter is full of the elements that have been advised against in a business letter. This is precisely because personal letters are personal and you are often talking to people with whom you have built up a relationship over the years. You know and understand the person and the type of language that is acceptable, therefore the use of clichés, jargon and so on is perfectly acceptable.

In many ways, the personal letter is the opposite of the business letter in that, in the business letter, you are trying to portray a positive image, well constructed and to the point with the express aim of communicating your message in a formal way.

You would certainly never handwrite a business letter, or finish by saying 'cheers'.

In some cases, with a personal letter, you may wish to adopt a mix of formal and personal. If you were writing to your Uncle Tom, who you have not seen for twenty years, you would not be writing in a very chummy style and yet you would not be over-personal either. You would use some elements of intimacy connected with the family and family memories but you would also be looking to present a rather formal image as you do not know this person well enough to adopt a chummy approach.

The art and craft of writing personal letters very much depends on you as a person, the person you are communicating to and also what you are trying to say. If you are in correspondence with a friend or acquaintance who is interested in politics and you are discussing political events then you would probably need to be well versed in the language and grammar, as well as current affairs, to be able to express yourself effectively.

If you are discussing matters of the heart then you would need to be possessed of a language and style that allowed you to express yourself sensitively. In many cases, the advantage of knowing the English language, and the ability to express your self, bringing into play all the elements of language, such as grammar and punctuation, will prove to be a great asset. It is hoped that the brief introduction contained within this book will assist that process.

Now read the key points from Chapter 9 overleaf.

Key points from Chapter 9

■ Personal letters have a different starting point to business letters.

■ Although personal letters are less formal than business letters, there are still formal conventions to be followed.

■ The personal letter will differ to the business letter in that the writer will normally put their name and address on the right hand side.

■ The letter will finish with a variety of different endings depending who you are writing to.

10

Editing and Proofreading

Editing and proofreading letters is perhaps one of the most important elements in the production of effective letters, whether business or personal.

An effective editor/proof reader will need a range of skills, including a sound knowledge of the English language and of the intricacies of grammar. This book has, hopefully, allowed the reader to absorb the basic structure of the language.

You should always allow time for proof reading and understand that the task is part of the process of producing a letter.

Focussing on proof reading

Many environments are not ideal for proofreading so you should try to find a space where you can work comfortably without interruption. If your letter is complex or technical you may prefer to enlist some help to read the 'dead' copy (first draft) while you concentrate on producing the live (original) copy. Proof reading is about detail. However, we need to be aware of the broader impression of the piece of writing. You should proof read for:

- visual impression
- sense of the message
- accuracy of the detail.

Visual impression

What does the page look like? Is there too much detail on the page and is there enough white space? Is the page balanced between top and bottom and if there is a large gap at the bottom is this intended? Is the text justified? Is it aligned to the left only? Are headings too large or small and is the size of typeface appropriate?

Reading for sense

This aspect can test your knowledge of grammar and ability to write clearly.

Are the paragraph breaks in the right place and are sentences too long? Is there enough variety in the sentence structure? Are there errors of grammar and is the word order correct? Is the message of the letter clear?

Reading for detail

You should expect to find errors at the start of the text and near other errors. In addition, errors will appear in common words which are usually mixed up, such as:

- not/no
- there/the
- and/an

Errors will also appear when repeating from the end of a line to the beginning of the next line, in changes from standard type and in changes of page formation: margins, columns etc.

It is easy to rationalise these errors. Changes of type or page formation cause us to think about control instructions rather than the flow of typing. Some word processing software will not show the end of one line and the beginning of the next line simultaneously on the monitor.

You will be reassured by the relative ease with which you will find errors such as omitted letters, spaces, punctuation marks or substitutions of one letter for another. You will also be aware of the need to concentrate carefully when you proof read a letter properly You should ensure that you proof read a letter twice to ensure that you have not missed mistakes.

Check you are clear and concise

No single aspect of your writing will produce a clear, concise style: you will need to review a number of elements.

Sequence
- check that your letter achieves a progression of ideas
- see that you move from where you are at the start to where you want to be at the end.

Paragraphs

A paragraph that might suit a long report can look excessive when applied to another letter:

- make paragraphs in letters relatively short
- make the topic of each paragraph clear
- if you have divided a paragraph, see that the new paragraph has a clear headline and is not left dangling by a pronoun.

Sentences

- check your sentence length
- aim for an average of twenty words but vary your sentence length for interest.

102

- Remember that a series of short sentences can read like a menu.

Punctuation

- see that punctuation properly supports the structure of your writing.
- Be sure the reader will absorb the meaning in a single reading.
- If the punctuation is struggling to reveal your meaning rewrite the sentence

Active voice

- link subject and verb directly by presenting your case in the active voice.

Familiar words

- use familiar words that will be comfortable for the reader

Concrete words

- use concrete words to paint a clear picture for the reader.
- Make your specification explicit and complete

Cliches

- avoid over- used business expressions
- use your own words to set the right tone and help a flow of ideas.

Jargon

- Use jargon to tune in to the reader
- Avoid jargon that will sound out of tune.

Fulfil your aim

Ask yourself key questions:
- who will read my letter?
- What does my reader need to know?
- What did I need to know?
- Is the required action clear?
- Will the reader know when to respond?

Proof reading and editing is an important skill and it is essential that letters are read and amended as necessary. Treat your first letter as a first draft that will need fine-tuning before you send it. If you are writing a particularly emotive letter, sometimes it is better to sleep on it for a night rather than send it immediately. Now read the key points from chapter 10 overleaf.

Key points from Chapter 10

■ Editing and proofreading is one of the most important elements when writing a letter, particularly a business letter.

■ An effective proof-reader will need a range of skills, including a sound knowledge of the English language.

■ Proof reading is about detail.

■ In addition to detail you should be aware of the broader impression of a piece of writing, such as visual impression, sense of message and accuracy of detail.

11

Writing Effective emails

In the previous chapters, we have covered business and personal letters. In this chapter we will cover business emails and also e mails that cover job applications and also marketing emails.

Business emails

In many cases now, whereas once upon a time a letter was necessary to confirm a deal or to agree on a business deal, now it is quite common to use an e mail. Because email is a rather different form of correspondence then it follows that there are slightly different rules to follow.

Although emails are often seen as less formal than printed business letters, in the business world you cannot afford to let your language appear to be informal. Email may be faster and more efficient, but your client or business partner will not easily forgive correspondence that is too casual.

Begin with a greeting

It's important to always open your email with a greeting, such as "Dear Peter,". Depending on the formality of your relationship, you may want to use their family name as opposed to their given name, i.e. "Dear Mrs. Davies,". If the relationship is more casual, you can simply say, "Hi Susan," If you're contacting a company, not an individual, you may write "To Whom It May Concern:" Thank the recipient If you are replying to a client's inquiry, you should begin with a line of thanks. For example, if someone has a question about your company, you can say, "Thank you for contacting (XXX) Company."

If someone has replied to one of your emails, be sure to say, "Thank you for your prompt reply." or "Thanks for getting back to me." If you can find any way to thank the reader, then do. It will put him or her at ease, and it will make you appear more courteous.

State your purpose

If, however, you are initiating the email communication, it may be impossible to include a line of thanks. Instead, begin by stating your purpose. For example, "I am writing to enquire about ..." or "I am writing in reference to ..." It's important to make your purpose clear early on in the email, and then move into the main text of your email.

Good Grammar!

Remember to pay careful attention to grammar, spelling and punctuation, and to avoid run-on sentences by keeping your sentences short and clear.

Closing remarks

Before you end your email, it's polite to thank your reader one more time as well as add some courteous closing remarks. You might start with "Thank you for your patience and cooperation." or "Thank you for your consideration." and then follow up with, "If you have any questions or concerns, don't hesitate to let me know." and "I look forward to hearing from you." End with a closing The last step is to include an appropriate closing with your name. "Best regards," "Sincerely," and "Thank you," are all professional. It's a good idea to avoid closings such as "Best wishes," or "Cheers," as these are best used in casual, personal emails. Finally, before you hit the send button, review and spell check your email one more time to make sure it's truly perfect! -

The following are some tips to help you when you are writing business letters through email.

o A heading is not necessary in an email (your return address, their address, and the date).

o Use a descriptive subject line.

o Avoid using an inappropriate or silly email address; register a professional sounding address if you don't have one.

o Use simple formatting, keep everything flush with the left margin; avoid special formatting and tabs.

o Keep your letter formal, just because it's an email instead of a hard copy is no excuse for informality (don't forget to use spell check and proper grammar).

o Try to keep your letter less than 80 characters wide, some email readers will create line breaks on anything longer and ruin the formatting.

o If possible, avoid attachments unless the recipient has requested or is expecting an attachment. If it is a text document, simply cut and paste the text below your letter and strip out any special formatting.

o If the person's name is unknown, address the person's title e.g. Dear Director of Human Resources.

Job application emails

As with business emails, it is now common to email companies with CV's, job applications and cover letters. Your covering email is quite important as this is quite often the first thing that a prospective employer might see. First impressions can be lasting impressions!

Subject line

After you have checked that you have the right email address, you need to make sure that you put the right information in the subject line. This immediately shows the respondent what the email is about and ensures that it does not get overlooked or counted as spam.

Addressing the email

In the same way as a covering letter, a covering email should be addressed to the right person as outline don the job specification. Be sure to address the recipient in the correct manner, either as 'Mr' or 'Mrs' or 'Ms' (if you are not sure of status). If the job specification simply states 'S. Wilson' then just address sit S Wilson as guessing can be quite insulting if you get it wrong.

If you are applying for a job that requires an initial covering letter then it is a good idea to keep your email short and to the point. One paragraph is enough which should act as an introduction to you as a person, what you can bring to the company in question and why you are applying for the position.

Attachments

If you need to attach your CV and covering letter to your email, there are a few things that you need to be wary about. Firstly, make sure that your documents are named correctly.-simply calling your CV 'CV' isn't very descriptive, especially when your potential employer is likely to be drowning in them. make sure you include your name when naming your documents and be sure to actually attach them to your email before sending. Its surprising how many people forget!

When signing off your email, you should try to end with something positive and polite like; "Thank you for taking the time to review my application. I look forward to hearing from you". This will show that you are enthusiastic and polite, two attributes that all employers want to see.

Also be sure to sign off with "Kind Regards" or "Yours Sincerely" rather than something chatty or informal.
Taking time over your email should help you in your quest for a job. First impressions, lasting impressions!

Email marketing

According to some estimates, more than 144 billion emails are sent every day—and, sometimes, it seems like every one of them lands in your inbox. We all know what it's like to be bombarded with email messages—all competing for a share of our attention during a busy day.

There are certain rules to adopt when using emails for the purpose of marketing. As we all know, marketing emails can seem annoying and irrelevant. We delete them more often than not. There is also the problem of spam and what it might do to your computer. Below are a few tips to help you construct an effective marketing e mail which might get read.

If it's your job to come up with a subject line that is compelling enough to cut through all that clutter, it's a good idea to apply your experience as an email recipient to help you craft the perfect subject line. What gets your attention? How do you decide which emails to trash unopened and which to read? Scores of scientific studies can tell you which words appear with the most frequency in successful email campaigns. And that is useful information. But in creating a compelling subject line, sometimes a simple strategy works best.

Keep it brief

When prospects are scanning their inboxes, a short, snappy subject is more likely to catch their eye than a lengthier line. If possible, it's best to keep the subject line short enough to appear as one line on a smaller device screen, such as a smartphone or tablet. Keep it short and sweet to improve your open and rates.

Don't waste valuable space

A subject line doesn't provide much space, so make every word count. Don't waste space with words (such as "hello") that don't add much value to your message. When crafting your subject line, evaluate each word and make sure it adds value—from the standpoint of providing information or encouraging readers to open the email.

Be specific

When readers are scanning new messages in their inbox, they're generally in a hurry to respond to urgent messages or tackle the next task in their busy day. In such a state of mind, they won't have much patience for mystery. Cut to the chase by using the subject line to tell them what the message is about.

Make it searchable

There's a good chance your reader won't have time to focus on your message when they first see it, so it's wise to give them an easy way to return to the message when they have more time. If you make the subject line searchable so readers can easily find it later, there's a better chance that they'll revisit your email, even if they don't have time at first.

Include a call to action

Make sure your subject line tells the reader what he or she can do to benefit from the message—whether that's to visit a site, make a call, or just read the message. A brief line that summarizes the value can be highly effective, so think about what's in it for the reader and try to convey that in the subject line.

Don't create anxiety

Although you want your readers to take action, it's important to balance a call to action with a signal that you respect their time. Subject lines that include phrases such as "immediate response required" can come across as arrogant. Adding "FYI" or "no need to reply" can take the pressure off while still signalling that the message contains valuable information.

Include your company name

Readers will be more likely to open an email if they know who it's from and if they perceive value from the sending organization. Email is one of the major ways how we communicate in business. The issue isn't email itself, but inbox overload and finding a way to separate the mundane and annoying from the truly important. There are proven ways to tame overflowing inboxes, and every professional needs a sound strategy. Your challenge as an email marketer is to ensure that your message makes the cut.

****

12

Hints on Texting Business Colleagues and Clients

Texting and other forms of electronic communications are on the rise, both personal texts and in the workplace. So, in the workplace when is it appropriate to text a colleague.

Texting a colleague generally depends on how casual your relationship is, what you're texting the person about and what this person's seniority level is. Texting is fairly personal, indeed, our phones have become an extension of our personalities to some degree, and texting a form of direct messaging. The problem with texting, however, is that it can lose context. When texting a colleague, you should consider the following rules of etiquette.

1. Texting your manager

Texting your manager has become increasingly necessary, especially when an issue is urgent or needs to be resolved quickly. When you do text, you should be communicating simple messages such as meeting times and places. Or text when the message requires an immediate response or requests a coffee meeting. Never text bad news about a contract, an important decisions or a message that includes abbreviations. Everything should be kept professional. Of course, you should always respond to any inquiries your manager texts to you.

If the manager is younger and/or running a small business, texting language may be more colloquial. If you're not sure, refer to your corporate communications policy.

2. Texting team members

In general, you should be cautious when texting team members. These messages may depend on age, gender, personal relationship and even hours. Everything you write might be relayed to other team members and to managers. Screenshots can be taken of everything you write and passed on, then taken out of context. When in doubt, be professional.

Take into consideration your recipients' relationship status and emotional state, and remember that texts lose context. These messages can also be misconstrued by your significant others and cause problems at home, even if they're an inside joke.

Try not to text team members after working hours unless you have a personal relationship with them outside of work. If you feel like you want to text them about work after 5 pm, use email.

Texting your prospective client

This is a hotly debated topic in the sales community in particular. Texting your prospective client is dependent on the type of rapport you have, whether this individual has given permission and where in the sales process you are. Never cold-call through text messaging. Many people believe that text messaging is still a personal communication that requires urgent attention, and that texting people you're soliciting business from when you don't know them is considered gauche.

If however you have a good rapport with your prospect, texting during business hours can be appropriate if it's about finding a meeting place, notifying this person that you are running late to a meeting, following up to a question or providing something of value. Being pushy about closing a deal using a text is not recommended.

Texting networking colleagues

For the most part, networking colleagues whom you're exchanging business information with can be fair game. Starting with email is traditional, typically. But people who are networking may be excited about helping each another with business development. So this relationship often escalates to texting fairly quickly. Once again, your texting relationship depends on gender and age. Younger members of the same sex are more likely to find it appropriate.

How to encourage less texting

Is texting making you or your colleagues angry? Want to encourage fewer texts to your phone after hours? Here are some tips to decrease texts and keep your mobile phone free of business during your personal time:

- Stop including your mobile phone on your business cards
- Convey your own communication policy in your email signature. Exclude your mobile phone and add a line specifically requesting, *Please send all correspondence via email.*
- Ask those contacting you to communicate only during business hours, and if they need to send you work, to send it only through email. Entrepreneurs and freelancers may forget that others aren't working at their odd hours.
- For major offenders, start using the Do Not Disturb feature on your cell phone during the weekends and evenings.

Walk into any boardroom two minutes before a meeting and you'll find the same scenario: a table full of executives checking their phones with their heads bowed in the "smartphone prayer."

Summary

Text messaging is the fastest way to communicate in business. Quicker than email and more convenient than a phone call, it's become commonplace. But it's not always the best choice.

Choose to text messages for simple notifications or reminders like "I'm running five minutes late," or "Remember to bring the report." As a general rule, consider texting only appropriate for a maximum of two messages -- one message and one reply.

Here are five rules to avoid a text message business blunder.

1. Keep it positive.

Like email, the tone of a text message can be misinterpreted by the recipient. Quick messages can make you come off as flippant or harsh. Instead of staccato phrases, write complete sentences. Add polite touches like "please" and "thank you." Re-read every message before pressing send to double-check your tone

2. Avoid serious topics.

You wouldn't break up with your girlfriend over a text message --
to be clear, you should not -- and the same goes for business.
Never give negative feedback or fire someone via a text message.
Any serious conversation should take place face-to-face. It allows
for subtle interaction through facial expressions and will ensure
clear communication.

3. Don't abbreviate every other word.

Abbreviations are common in casual texts, but you should be
careful how often you use them. Common abbreviations like
"LOL" (laugh out loud) and "np" (no problem) are safe choices.
However, if you're communicating with a new customer or
acquaintance, take 30 extra seconds and type out each word.

Avoid informal shortcuts like "u" (you) and less common
abbreviations like "SMH" (shaking my head) or "MFW" (my face
when). Don't leave your clients and colleagues confused; your
texts should convey messages quickly and clearly.

4. Don't text a last-minute cancellation.

There are a thousand reasons someone may miss a text message.
Don't depend on a quick note to cancel a meeting or change a

lunch venue. For an important or time-sensitive message, pick up the phone.

5. Double-check the autocorrect.

Smart phones can occasionally be a little too smart. Autocorrect and voice-to-text features have a sneaky way of changing your intended message into something entirely different and often embarrassing. When using voice-to-text, ensure you're in a quiet location. It picks up on background noise and may type a nearby conversation instead of what you're saying.

****

Glossary of terms

Acronym. A word formed from the initial letters of other words.

Adjective. A word that describes a noun.

Adverb. A word that qualifies a verb, an adjective or other adverb.

Clause, dependent. A main group of words containing a verb that depends on the main clause. They cannot stand alone.

Conjunction. A word that links two main clauses together.

Gerund. A present participle used as a noun.

Inverted commas. Speech marks put around speech and quotations.

Jargon. Words or expressions used by a certain group of people.

Justify. Adjust margins so that they are level.

Metaphor. An implied comparison of two things.

Noun, abstract. A word that denotes a quality or state.

Noun, collective. A singular word which refers to a group of people or things.

Noun, common. The name of a thing.

Noun, proper. The name of a person or place. It always begins with a capital letter.

Object. A noun or pronoun that follows the verb and is related to the subject.

Paragraph. A group of sentences dealing with the same topic.

Personify. Giving a humane object human characteristics.

Phrase. A group of words not necessarily containing a verb or making sense on its own.

Preposition. A word that governs a noun or pronoun.

Pronoun, interrogative. A pronoun that is used at the start of a question.

Pronoun, personal. A word that takes the place of a noun.

Pronoun, relative. This has a similar role to a conjunction. It joins clauses together but is closely linked to a noun.

Simile. A comparison of two things using 'like' or 'as'.

Subject. The noun or pronoun on which the rest of the clause depends.

Synonym. A word that can be used to replace another.

Tautology. A statement that is repeated in a different way in the same sentence.

Thesaurus. A book which will give a collection of synonyms.

****

Index

****

www.straightforwardco.co.uk

All titles, listed below, in the Straightforward Guides Series can be purchased online, using credit card or other forms of payment by going to www.straightfowardco.co.uk A discount of 25% per title is offered with online purchases.

Law

A Straightforward Guide to:

Consumer Rights
Bankruptcy Insolvency and the Law
Employment Law
Private Tenants Rights
Family law
Small Claims in the County Court
Contract law
Intellectual Property and the law
Divorce and the law
Leaseholders Rights
The Process of Conveyancing
Knowing Your Rights and Using the Courts
Producing Your own Will
Housing Rights
The Bailiff the law and You
Probate and The Law

Company law

What to Expect When You Go to Court

Guide to Competition Law

Give me Your Money-Guide to Effective Debt Collection

Caring for a Disabled Child

General titles

Letting Property for Profit

Buying, Selling and Renting property

Buying a Home in England and France

Bookkeeping and Accounts for Small Business

Creative Writing

Freelance Writing

Writing Your own Life Story

Writing performance Poetry

Writing Romantic Fiction

Speech Writing

Teaching Your Child to Read and write

Teaching Your Child to Swim

Raising a Child-The Early Years

Creating a Successful Commercial Website

The Straightforward Business Plan

The Straightforward C.V.

Successful Public Speaking

Handling Bereavement

Individual and Personal Finance
Understanding Mental Illness
The Two Minute Message
Tiling for Beginners

Go to: www.straightforwardco.co.uk

MANAGING ASTHMA
IN PRIMARY CARE

Antony Crockett

OXFORD

Blackwell Scientific Publications

LONDON EDINBURGH BOSTON

MELBOURNE PARIS BERLIN VIENNA

©1993 by
Blackwell Scientific Publications
Editorial Offices:
Osney Mead, Oxford OX2 OEL
25 John Street, London WC1N 2BL
23 Ainslie Place, Edinburgh EH3 6AJ
238 Main Street, Cambridge
  Massachusetts 02142, USA
54 University Street, Carlton
  Victoria 3053, Australia

Other Editorial Offices:
Librairie Arnette SA
2, rue Casimir-Delavigne
75006 Paris
France

Blackwell Wissenschafts-Verlag GmbH
Düsseldorfer Str. 38
D-10707 Berlin
Germany

Blackwell MZV
Feldgasse 13
A-1238 Wien
Austria

First published 1993

Set by Alden Multimedia, Northampton
Printed and bound in Great Britain
at the Alden Press, Oxford

DISTRIBUTORS

Marston Book Services Ltd
PO Box 87
Oxford OX2 ODT
(*Orders:* Tel: 0865 791155
        Fax: 0865 791927
        Telex: 837515)

USA
Blackwell Scientific Publications, Inc.
238 Main Street
Cambridge, MA 02142
(*Orders:* Tel: 800 759-6102
        617 876-7000)

Canada
Times Mirror Professional Publishing, Ltd
130 Flaska Drive
Markham, Ontario L6G 1B8
(*Orders:* Tel: 800 268-4178
        416 470-6739)

Australia
Blackwell Scientific Publications Pty Ltd
54 University Street
Carlton, Victoria 3053
(*Orders:* Tel: 03 347-5552)

A catalogue record for this title
is available from the British Library

ISBN 0-632-03757-1

A catalogue record for this title
is available from the Library of Congress

MANAGING ASTHMA
IN PRIMARY CARE

CONTENTS

PREFACE

Asthma is a subject often in the news. Those in Primary Care are criticized frequently and exhorted to do better by colleagues, politicians and the public. Recent changes in clinic payments and the publication of sets of guidelines have further confused many of us. This book provides a simple, practical guide on how asthma can be managed effectively in general practice.

Asthma is a common, incurable disease. It affects people of all ages and in all walks of life. Everyone knows someone who has asthma. Its effects are variable and occasionally unpredictable. All health workers are aware of how asthma can affect people's lives, and therefore all health workers should be familiar with the principles and goals of successful management. Until a cure is found, which still seems unlikely, all health workers must try to improve the quality of life of asthmatics. Only by good management can the health of all asthmatics improve.

Why another book about asthma? At times it may seem that the subject is over-publicized and is an example of empire building by sub-specialists. But it continues to be a subject of great interest not only in medical circles but also in the non-medical media. Asthma is now recognized by everyone as an increasingly common cause of illness and disability. The effects of the disease, or its treatment, cause much anxiety especially in parents of asthmatic children. Knowledge of asthma management by the public and health workers is patchy, despite the large amount of publicity given to it. How can this be? Ignorance and poor understanding give rise to myths and suspicions which ill-informed health workers find hard to refute. On the other hand, the volume and quality of much of the information available, by appearing over-complicated or elitist, may actually inhibit the least well-informed health workers who are most in need of encouragement.

This is the first book written specifically for all members of the primary health care team. The book does not pretend to be an academic text but is a practical guide on how proper asthma care can be delivered effectively.

Antony Crockett
May 1993

ACKNOWLEDGEMENTS

I would like to thank Beverley Whitewood and Julie El-Khatib for their skill and hard work in preparing the manuscript and my partners and especially my wife and children for indulging me with the time and energy I needed to write this book. Thanks too to the members of the Swindon Branch of the National Asthma Campaign for their helpful additions, to Glenys Talbot SRN for Chapter 3, and to Amanda Ryde from Blackwell Scientific Publications. I would like to thank the National Asthma Campaign for permission to use the Adult Management Plan.

Elm Tree Surgery   Antony Crockett
Shrivenham   *May 1993*
Swindon SN6 8AA

CHAPTER 1:
INTRODUCTION

Asthma is a common, chronic disease that affects people of all ages. Although there is no cure, there are a variety of effective management options, including some very effective medication. The principal objective means to assess asthma severity, the peak flow meter, is now available on prescription. There is widespread interest in asthma throughout general practice, including a special interest group for GPs, the General Practitioners in Asthma Group. There are well-publicized and accepted guidelines for the management of chronic asthma, recently revised by the British Thoracic Society in conjunction with the British Paediatric Association, the Research Unit of the Royal College of Physicians of London, the King's Fund Centre, the National Asthma Campaign, the Royal College of General Practitioners, the General Practitioners in Asthma Group, the British Association of Accident and Emergency Medicine and the British Paediatric Respiratory Group [1]. Asthma clinics in general practice, often run by nurses, are becoming much more common [2]. Why then does asthma still cause so much illness and affect the quality of so many lives, and why does the number of deaths from asthma show no sign of reducing?

Clearly, being diagnosed as an asthmatic and requiring prescribed treatment does not necessarily lead to the optimal quality of care. Increasing asthmatics' knowledge of their disease and its management has little effect by itself on illness. However, combining patient education with the widespread use of self-management plans, especially the use of peak flow meters, together with the increased emphasis on the importance of regular anti-inflammatory therapy, can and do reduce morbidity [3]. These measures should result in improved care for asthmatics.

This guide is intended to build on these platforms of good asthma care:

Platforms for good asthma care
- the frequent and informed review of asthmatics and their morbidity by practice-based asthma teams
- education of the asthmatic and their carers about the disease and its management

- the importance of regular anti-inflammatory therapy in the correct dose by the correctly used inhaler
- the use of peak flow monitoring and self-management plans by asthmatics
- the step-wise approach to chronic asthma management, according to the needs of the patient

Each platform is important and each inter-relates with the others. This guide aims to provide some background information about asthma in an easily understood way that can be shared by the primary health care team involved in the care of asthmatics and by the asthmatics themselves. The management of asthma, including drug treatments, is discussed in some depth.

Setting up and running the clinic are discussed next, with guidelines on how to do so and also on what to say to asthmatics and what they should all eventually know. The importance of listening and of forming a partnership to share the management of the disease between professional carers and asthmatics is emphasized. Finally there is a brief discussion on audit, with the results of an actual audit which, it is hoped, will stimulate practices to perform their own.

Who this book is for

The Practice Nurse: most general practice asthma clinics are nurse and doctor, or mainly nurse-run. Practice nurses are well suited to the task as they are as good if not better than doctors at following protocols, talking and listening to patients [4]. Nurses obviously need education, training and support and this book hopes to provide all of these, however, it cannot replace the need for further training either through the local postgraduate centre or specialist centres, such as the Asthma Training Centre in Stratford. The support of one or more general practitioner colleagues within the practice is essential and a prerequisite for the nurse before attempting to run a clinic. Further support may come via a Family Health Service Authority or Health Board facilitator, local nurse tutors, pharmaceutical companies, the National Asthma Campaign, and indirectly from the General Practitioners in Asthma Group.

The General Practitioner: for those who already have an interest in asthma it is hoped that this book will become the stimulus to channel the interest into action and start up an asthma clinic; for those with little or no interest in asthma, this may be the spark that lights the flames of interest. Support and education can be obtained from the sources outlined above, as well as the Royal College of General Practitioners, the British Paediatric Association and the Royal College of Physicians.

The Practice Manager and Receptionist may like to browse through the book, perhaps concentrating on the Clinic and Audit sections. Understanding by ancillary staff of their medical and nursing colleagues' roles and aspirations will help nurture teamwork and group loyalty. They can also help by monitoring repeat prescription requests and by encouraging face-to-face contact between the nurse or doctor and the patient.

The Community Nurse, School Nurse and Health Visitor will also derive increased professional satisfaction from sharing in their colleagues' aims and objectives and becoming part of a team.

The Community Pharmacist: most pharmacists have a reactive role in health care. An alert, informed and caring pharmacist is in a good position to check and advise on drug compliance, inhaler technique, peak flow technique and monitoring and can encourage attendance at the asthma clinic, especially by identifying those asthmatics who may not be well controlled. If pharmacists can share in the knowledge and objectives of their medical and nursing colleagues they will be able to use their skills more appropriately and satisfactorily, and can often help in the instigation, execution and reinforcement of practice protocols and policies for asthma, thereby playing a valuable role as members of the health care team.

How to use this book

This book is intended mainly to encourage the development of asthma clinics in general practice run by a primary health care team. The book should be read by all, and used as a basis upon which to build the asthma care appropriate for each patient. It will then act as a point of reference rather than a complete handbook. It is hoped that the book will educate and stimulate as well as act as a reference source.

Objectives of this book

The objectives of the book are to stimulate and encourage so that:

1 Every asthmatic will be diagnosed, and both the asthmatic and the practice are aware of the diagnosis.

2 Every practice will successfully and effectively manage the vast majority of asthmatics within the practice.

3 Every patient feels confident of managing their asthma, and that every asthmatic feels confident of the management advised by their practice.

4 Every practice runs an asthma clinic.

5 Every clinician uses the resources, especially drugs and hospitals effectively and efficiently.

6 Each practice sees a reduction in morbidity and mortality due to asthma.

7 Everyone involved in the care of asthma enjoys what they do, finds it stimulating and rewarding, and acquires the enthusiasm to teach others.

CHAPTER 2: ASTHMA AND ITS MANAGEMENT

2.1 ASTHMA—THE DISEASE

Introduction

Asthma is a common chronic disease affecting people of all ages. It is the cause of much illness and many deaths. Fortunately there are a number of effective treatments which can both relieve symptoms and prevent asthma attacks. This makes it a particularly rewarding chronic disease to manage. Successful management may result in fewer deaths and a greatly improved quality of life for all asthmatics, and fewer asthma emergencies.

History of asthma care

The word asthma derives from a Greek word meaning to breathe hard. Asthma was recognized nearly 4000 years ago in China and was treated with leaves of the plant *Ephedra* [1]. It was not until the 1920s that ephedrine was first used in Western medicine. Hippocrates described asthma and recognized that it could be fatal. By the sixteenth century feather pillows, dust and changes in the weather were noted to affect asthmatics [1]. The lack of effective treatment however led to the misconception that asthma was a psychologically based illness and until the mid-twentieth century it was accepted teaching that asthma was a nervous illness that was rarely fatal.

Since the late 1950s there has been increasing research into the causes, pathology and treatment of asthma. Advances made in the details of lung physiology and pathology, together with advances in applied pharmacology, have led us to our present state of knowledge.

Definition

The definition of asthma causes more discussion and disagreement than most aspects of the disease, especially amongst academics.

The International Consensus Report on Diagnosis and Management has defined asthma as a chronic inflammatory disorder of the airways in which many cells play a role, including mast cells and eosinophils. In susceptible individuals this inflammation causes

5

symptoms which are usually associated with widespread but variable airflow obstruction that is often reversible either spontaneously or with treatment, and causes an associated increase in airway responsiveness to a variety of stimuli [2].

Any definition of asthma must be simple and must be applicable, with few false positives or negatives. It is useless having a definition based only on the immunological changes seen in the bronchial mucosa if such changes are impossible to verify except by a few specialists. The definition below is, above all, simple.

> **Definition**
> Asthma is defined as a disease of the respiratory system involving inflammation of the airways and reversible symptoms of bronchospasm.

One of the problems of defining asthma is that it is not a single entity but a term used to describe a set of symptoms which result from the action of a number of incompletely understood mechanisms. The common factors are the hyper-reactive nature of the airways which respond to a wide variety of stimuli; the reversibility of the airway narrowing; and the intermittent nature of the symptoms.

Prevalence

Asthma is a common disease throughout the world. Prevalence rates do vary markedly between different countries, accounted for in part by differing diagnostic approaches [3]. A popular figure for the prevalence of asthma in the UK is 5% of adults and 10% of children [4], although recent surveys indicate that over 10% of children [5,6,7] and 7% of adults [8,9] will receive a diagnosis of asthma in their lifetime. This means that there are about 2.5 million asthmatics requiring surveillance and management. In children the prevalence rates obtained from studies in different locations in the UK vary from 8% to 15% [10]. The prevalence seems to be increasing in the UK [6,7,8] and also in other countries such as Canada [11], Australia [12] and New Zealand [13]. In adults, males and females are about equally affected; in children the ratio of males to females is about 2:1.

Age of onset

Asthma is more common in children, and affects about 10% of children in the UK [8]. Most asthmatics have an age of onset before 10 years old. Asthma can first present at any age, but most commonly in childhood and in the fourth and fifth decades [14]. Symptoms develop in 50% of asthmatic children by the age of three and in 80% by the age of five years.

Pathophysiology

The primary abnormality in asthma is thought to be a hypersensitive bronchial tree. In susceptible individuals the lining of the bronchial tree becomes over-sensitive to the stimuli applied to it. The susceptibility of an individual is probably genetically inherited. This susceptibility appears to be switched on or exaggerated by certain environmental factors such as exposure to allergens or irritants [15].

Allergens

An allergen is a substance capable of eliciting an exaggerated response of the body when the body is exposed to it, leading to disease. Allergic asthma is becoming more common; this may be related to changes in the home environment, exposure to environmental pollutants such as ozone and cigarette smoke, ingestion of chemical additives, changes in farming practices, childhood infection or to any combination of these and other factors. One of the most common allergens in the UK is the house dust mite (specifically, its faeces). These tiny creatures eat shed human skin scales, and they live, breed, excrete and die in our homes. They especially like foam-backed carpets and a square metre of this may house 1.5 million mites. House dust mites and their waste make up one-third of all dust from carpets and a feather pillow may contain 60 million mites weighing 90 g [16]. The concentration of mite allergens in most UK homes has increased fourfold in the last 10 years [17]. Identifying allergy is best done clinically. Skin prick tests and IgE measurements may be used to help in diagnosis or management.

The mechanism

The combination of a sensitized lung lining and exposure to an allergen results in inflammation of the lung lining. Different asthmatics may be sensitive to different allergens. Most asthmatics will also be sensitive to other, non-allergen triggers, such as cold air, particulate irritants, emotion and exercise. Some asthmatics' sensitivity will vary over time and with different combinations of triggers.

Whatever the trigger, the mechanism is the same. Bronchoconstriction occurs, possibly as a protective response to limit further inhalation of allergens or irritants. If this is sustained for any length of time, the sensitized lining of the lung, especially in medium-sized bronchi and bronchioles, will become inflamed and oedematous. In atopic asthma the effect is caused by specific allergens (as detailed above) linking with their specific antibodies resulting in degranulation of mast cells and other cells, which results in the release of various local hormones and mediator substances. In non-atopic asthma this stage is less well understood. In all cases the inflammatory stages are characterized by oedema of the bronchial mucosa and increased bronchial secretions. This in turn leads to increased irritability of the bronchial smooth muscle. The net effect is increased resistance to airflow. In certain cases exposure to inducers that result in inflammation of the bronchi with associated airway narrowing and hyper-responsiveness will be more prominent. In other cases, exposure to inciters that precipitate acute constriction with less of an inflammatory response will be prominent [18]. If the asthma is persistent and under-treated the smooth muscle will eventually hypertrophy and irreversible anatomical changes may occur in the small airways. One of the aims of current asthma management is the prevention of chronic anatomical changes that may otherwise occur even in the so-called mild asthmatic. It is hoped, but not yet proven, that this may be achieved by effective anti-inflammatory treatments.

The underlying pathology of asthma in pre-school children may differ from older subjects. Bronchial hyper-reactivity is not a significant feature in such children. Similarly there is no evidence that chronic inflammation is the basis for the episodic asthma associated with viral infections.

Types

Asthma can be classified by aetiology and by severity [19]. Using the classification by aetiology, there are two main types; extrinsic and intrinsic, although the distinction between these two is not always clear-cut and may in some cases be of little clinical relevance. Extrinsic asthma is characterized by an allergic response to identifiable specific triggers, such as pollen, moulds, dust, animal danders and drugs. Some extrinsic asthma involves a specific IgE-mediated reaction and is associated with a genetic predisposition to allergies such as asthma, eczema, hayfever and urticaria—this is called atopy. Intrinsic asthma is characterized by non-allergic mechanisms in response to non-specific or unknown triggers such as cold air. Some triggers may be common to all types of asthma, such as upper respiratory tract infections and exercise. When classifying untreated asthma by severity, three main categories are used [18]: mild, moderate and severe. These form a continuous spectrum, and patients may change categories over time. Mild asthma results in intermittent, brief symptoms. Mild asthmatics have peak flow readings of at least 80% predicted with less than 20% variability, and they require minimal symptomatic treatment taken as needed. Moderate asthmatics have exacerbations once or twice a week, with nocturnal symptoms more frequently, and symptoms on most days. Their peak flow readings are only 60–80% predicted but return to normal or near normal after using a bronchodilator. Their peak flow variability may be up to 30%. They require anti-inflammatory treatment on a regular basis.

Severe asthmatics have daily symptoms with frequent nocturnal symptoms and frequent exacerbations. Their physical activities are curtailed and they may have had life-threatening exacerbations or required hospital admission in the past. Their peak flow will be less than 60% predicted with more than 30% variability and will not achieve predicted levels despite optimal therapy. They require daily preventative and relieving treatments and may need frequent courses of oral steroids.

Jenkins [20] categorized 63% of asthmatics as mild, 29% as moderate and 8% as severe; in practice the severity of many asthmatics' disease is very variable and some asthmatics may change categories very rapidly. Modern management aims for all asthmatics to receive sufficient and appropriate treatment so that they become symptom-free.

The severity of an individual's asthma can be assessed to some extent by the amount and type of treatment required to keep them symptom-free and with normal peak flow readings. This is discussed more fully on pp. 37–39.

Clinical features

Symptoms

As asthma is a disease characterized by reversible airway narrowing, the clinical features of asthma show great variability both between asthmatics and in the individual over time. The primary problems are the sensitive bronchial mucosa and hyper-reactive bronchial muscle. The net effects of bronchial mucosal oedema, increased mucus production and smooth muscle spasm, lead to airway narrowing and cause the four main symptoms of asthma: cough, wheeze, shortness of breath and chest tightness. Certain symptoms may predominate at certain ages.

In adults

In adults the characteristic symptoms are wheezing and breathlessness. The severity of the symptoms varies greatly. These symptoms may be preceded or accompanied by chest tightness and a cough. Occasionally the cough may be productive of clear, green or yellow sputum. The sputum is usually a product of inflammation of the airways rather than infection.

In children

In children the symptoms may be similar, but a persistent cough, especially at night or after a cold, is common. There may be a history of repeated wheeze, again often at night. The symptoms are often precipitated by viral infections, exercise or excitement, allergens such as pets or dusts, cigarette smoke or family emotional disturbances. Some children are just slightly listless or non-specifically below par. Persistent or paroxysmal cough, especially if nocturnal, for more than 10–14 days, especially following a cold, is likely to be asthma and if recurrent should be considered as such until proved otherwise. Childhood wheezing is significantly associated with prematurity. This association is proportional to the degree of prematurity [21].

Signs

Physical signs during a severe acute exacerbation may include audible wheezing, tachycardia, tachypnoea, intercostal recession, the use of accessory muscles for breathing, distress and even cyanosis. Inability to talk in complete sentences is a sign of a severe attack. Chest auscultation will reveal an over-expanded chest with wheezing, or if very severe, a near silent chest. In between exacerbations there may be no abnormal findings at all.

Assessment

The severity of airflow obstruction is best assessed by measuring the ability of the patient to exhale air quickly from the lungs. The maximal flow rate is known as the peak flow and can be simply measured using a suitable meter. It is usually expressed as litres per minute (l/min) and normal ranges vary with age, sex and height. The reading will be decreased in proportion to the severity of the airway obstruction. Non-asthmatics' peak flow readings show very little variability and they have small reduction in peak flows with a cold and only minor increases in peak flow in response to bronchodilators.

The peak flow is a measure of airway narrowing. The narrowing can be reversed using drugs, and the peak flow will then return towards, or to, normal. Other chest diseases may produce symptoms similar to those of asthma and may cause the peak flow to drop.

Only in asthma, however, will it be possible to show a 20% or more variability in peak flow over the course of 24 hours; a fall in response to exposure to a trigger, and a rise again in response to treatment.

Use of the peak flow meter

Non-asthmatics and stable, well-controlled asthmatics will have peak flow readings consistently greater than 80% of that predicted. Less well-controlled asthmatics will have more variable peak flow readings, but the peak flow can be returned to within normal limits by treatment. Severe asthmatics will also have variable peak flow readings, which may not return to normal even after treatment. Non-asthmatics with certain other chest diseases may consistently have peak flow readings below 80% predicted despite treatment.

Many people, especially small children, cannot use a peak flow meter, so it is not a universally useful tool in diagnosing and managing asthma, but it is very useful if the asthmatic can use it.

Associated features

Features associated with asthma include other atopic manifestations such as allergic rhinitis (hayfever), allergic conjunctivitis, exogenous eczema and urticaria. Other associations include nasal polyps, chronic secretory otitis media, recurrent or chronic sinusitis and other catarrhal illnesses. Successful treatment or control of these associated features often greatly improves asthma control and is occasionally a prerequisite for successful asthma care [22,23].

The diagnosis of asthma (see Fig. 2.1)

History

Diagnosis is usually made on the history. There is often a family history of asthma, atopy or allergy which may act as a valuable pointer to the real cause of symptoms. Asthma may be in the patient's own, or family's, history but concealed as one of the many euphemisms:

wheezy bronchitis;
recurrent bronchitis;
a bad (or weak) chest;
prone to colds and coughs;
catarrh on the chest;
colds go to the chest.

Investigations

Clinical examination in between episodes may be normal, as may the peak flow. However, home recordings twice daily on waking and at 5–6 pm may show variability or a diurnal variation of more than 20%. Such a variation is usually diagnostic of asthma. Sometimes it is valuable to ask an individual who may be asthmatic to take peak flow readings at 5 minute intervals for 30 minutes after 10 minutes

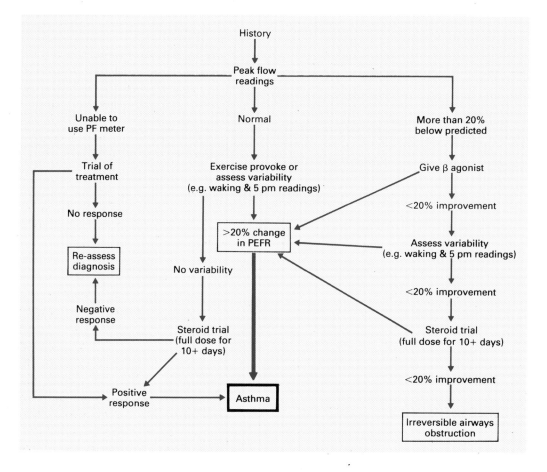

Fig. 2.1 The diagnosis of asthma.

of vigorous exercise. A fall in peak flow of over 20% would be diagnostic of asthma. A chest X-ray is mandatory if the symptoms and signs so warrant, or in the middle-aged or elderly smoker, especially on their first presentation. Most other tests are not usually helpful or necessary.

Therapeutic tests

Most workers use a trial of treatment in making the diagnosis, especially in children, often utilizing home peak flow monitoring if possible. If there is doubt about the reversibility of the airways obstruction, the ultimate therapeutic test is a two or three week course of oral steroids, 2 mg/kg for children or 30–60 mg for adults per day. Failure to relieve the symptoms or to increase the peak flow means the diagnostic test is negative and the person almost certainly does *not* have asthma. The trial is usually very well tolerated and is safe for the vast majority of people.

The effects of asthma on patients

Asthma is a very variable disease and ranges in severity from being nothing more than an occasional nuisance to being a severe life-threatening and life-dominating illness. It is relatively easy to measure the mortality from asthma, and some of the more obvious examples of morbidity, but it is harder to measure the subtle effects of asthma which may alter the quality of many asthmatics' lives. Asthma has an unacceptably high mortality and morbidity for such a common, well-researched disease for which there are such good, effective and safe treatments.

One of the aims of managing asthma is to abolish symptoms, and to allow asthmatics to lead a normal life, minimally troubled by the disease or its management. The reality is somewhat different. In the large 1990–91 National Asthma Survey [24] involving 61 000 respondents, Action Asthma found that nearly half the respondents experienced symptoms on most days and only a small minority had symptoms less frequently than once a fortnight. Most asthmatics are woken at least once a week by their symptoms and nearly 20% are woken every night. The knock-on effect from disturbed sleep is something of which most of us working in the caring professions are all too aware. Disturbed sleep in children may interfere with normal growth hormone secretion. A tired child may not fulfil their potential at school, neither will a tired adult at work. Indeed absenteeism due to asthma is a major problem with nearly 25% of asthmatics taking up to one week off a year [14]. This has social and economic consequences for the individual, the family and society as a whole. Remember that there are at least 2 million asthmatics in the UK. Amongst nine-year-old asthmatic children one in eight loses more than 30 days from school because of their disease [25], again with potentially grave consequences for their academic and developmental progress. Asthma symptoms can be very restrictive to leading a normal life style. Most patients believe that asthma restricts their daily lives, from avoiding smoky pubs to choice of holiday locations, selection of employment (if possible) or even where to live [24]. Physical activities are also curtailed in many asthmatics, from homework to playing with the children to gardening and sport. Twenty per cent of National Asthma Survey respondents thought asthma had a major effect on their lives, but many were so used to their restricted life style that they no longer regarded the restrictions as abnormal. While 74% of asthmatics maintain that asthma has at least a moderate effect on their lives, 37% of the partners of asthmatics and 38% of parents of asthmatic children maintain that asthma also affects their lives [26]. Thus the total number of people that asthma affects, directly or indirectly, may be over 3.5 million in the UK.

Mortality from asthma

Nearly 2000 people die from asthma every year in the UK [27]. However, there has been some doubt about the accuracy of some historical data on deaths from asthma [28,29]. Over one-third of these deaths occur in the under 65s, compared to less than 20% for all deaths. Asthma is thus an important source of lost potential life. Asthma mortality has stubbornly remained fairly static over the last 10 years despite improvements in its treatment and in knowledge of the disease.

The costs of asthma

The financial costs of asthma are considerable; the financial burden falls not only on the asthmatics themselves and their families, but also on the National Health Service (NHS), the Department of Social Security (sickness payments) and the economy in general (lost productivity).

NHS costs

The treatment of asthma cost the NHS at least £400 million in 1990, 20% of which was spent on hospital in-patient care.

The effect of asthma on NHS workload

The National Asthma Survey found that most asthmatics require and seek help only from their general practice, although 20% are seen at least once a year in hospital. In general practice, 10% of asthmatics received at least one night visit per year and 20% at least one day-time visit. About one-third of all asthmatics require either a home visit or emergency treatment in hospital each year. The hospital admission rates for asthma increased by 72% in the 1980s. It can be estimated that in 1992 about 100 000 asthmatics were hospitalized for asthma, 90 000 of whom would have been admitted as emergencies. About 30% of these admissions would have been children under the age of five.

Thus about 1.5–2 million asthmatics consult their general practitioners with asthma each year, generating 2.73 million general practitioner contacts at an estimated cost of at least £20 million. Medication for asthma, including dispensing fees, amounts to a further £225 million annually [30]. Referrals as hospital out-patients, assuming that 2.4% of GP consultations result in referral, would cost a further £7 million, including out-patient follow-up of previous in-patients [30].

Non NHS costs

The estimated total productivity foregone in 1990 by the 7.2 million working days lost due to asthma was £342 million. Of those working days, 5.7 million attracted Department of Social Security benefits at an additional cost of £60 million [30].

The effects and costs of asthma: summary

Thus asthma causes a variety of symptoms which affect a large number of people's ability to lead normal lives. Asthma places a considerable burden on the primary and secondary tiers of the NHS. It is still too frequent a cause of death, especially in the under 65s.

Prognosis

As stated earlier, at least 10% of children and 5% of adults are affected by asthma. Simple mathematics will show that not all childhood asthmatics have asthma as adults.

An incurable illness?

The symptoms of asthma are very variable over time and between individuals, so it is difficult to predict at an individual level whether the disease will continue to cause problems, become temporarily quiescent or disappear altogether. Recent developments in the understanding of the pathophysiological basis of asthma, especially the role of bronchial mucosal hyper-reactivity, have led most workers to accept that it is unlikely that an asthmatic can ever be said to be completely cured, but will always carry the potential to have asthma even if it never actually shows itself. On the other hand there are thousands of people who undoubtedly have had asthma in the past but have been symptom-free for decades.

Prognosis in children

The problem is particularly relevant to children with asthma. There are certain factors which will help with predicting which asthmatic children may 'grow out of it' [31].
1 If the age of onset is over 10 years, the prognosis is poor.
2 Multiple allergic manifestations are associated with poor prognosis.
3 The more severe the symptoms, the worse the prognosis.
4 Family history: if close relatives with childhood asthma 'grew out of it', the better the prognosis.
  It is sensible to continue follow-up and surveillance for at least two years after the last treatment needed or last asthmatic symptoms. It is also sensible to point out to patients and parents that symptoms may recur at any time in the future.

Some current concepts One of the most exciting prospects in treating asthma is the possibility of reducing the long-term lung damage that may occur in badly or under-treated asthma by using preventative or protective therapy. Poorly-treated or severe reversible obstructive airways disease (asthma) may eventually turn into irreversible obstructive airways disease (emphysema and chronic bronchitis) [32]. The long-term use of inhaled anti-inflammatory agents used to control asthma might halt this trend [33]. Another exciting theory is that early allergen exposure in susceptible infants results in their sensitization and the subsequent development of asthma. Vigorous treatment of such infants with high-dose inhaled steroids at first presentation might dampen or reduce the sensitization and inhibit the subsequent severity or chronicity of asthma [34,35,36], although this management is still at an experimental stage.

The aims of management

- to recognize asthma
- to abolish symptoms
- to restore normal or the best possible long-term airways function
- to minimize the risk of severe attack
- to enable normal growth in children
- to minimize absence from school or work

Compliance by the patient is essential. Its encouragement is an essential part of long-term management. Treatment must therefore be agreed with the patient.

All asthmatics are entitled to a full night's sleep, to exercise appropriately, to follow their chosen employment, to travel freely, to socialize normally and to have a cold with impunity.

Children should expect to grow and develop normally, taking part in all the activities every other child enjoys.

It may not always be possible to achieve every goal for every asthmatic. Nevertheless these aims should always be clearly agreed with the patient, with modifications as necessary for certain asthmatics.

Treatment is aimed at preventing exacerbations and protecting the lungs. Acute exacerbations – especially if requiring hospital admission, an out-of-hours consultation or nebulization – can usually be regarded as a failure of chronic management.

Preventative treatment should be the minimum which keeps the asthmatic symptom-free and able to live a normal life; relieving treatment should be whatever is necessary to allow the asthmatic to recover rapidly from an acute exacerbation.

Shared education   Every asthmatic and every carer should know about:

The disease: what is asthma, what triggers it, what to avoid.

The treatment: what is it, what does it do, what are the side-effects, how to take it, when to take it, what alternatives there are.

The exacerbation: how to recognize it, what to do, when to do it, when to call for help, how to call for help, what to do afterwards, how to prevent recurrence, how to monitor it.

The expectation: of a normal lifestyle, of best achievable peak flow and lung function, of normal life expectancy, of no progression to irreversible lung disease.

No asthmatic should smoke, either passively or, especially, actively.

Summary

Asthma is a very common chronic disease affecting people of all ages which can start at any age. It is characterized by a hypersensitive bronchial mucosa which readily becomes inflamed, causing swelling and oedema and increased mucus production. This inflammation may result in increased bronchial muscle irritability. The net result is an inflamed, narrowed airway with the symptoms of cough, wheeze, shortness of breath and chest tightness. The symptoms are reversible, and so are paroxysmal. The process may be provoked by exposure to certain stimuli. In most asthmatics the inflammatory response predominates, in a few the inflammatory response may be minimal and the bronchospastic response predominates [18].

Asthma is a very common cause of illness ranging from mild, post coryzal coughs to life-threatening disease. It is a cause of premature death and costs individuals and the nation a great deal. Asthma is incurable but fortunately there are a variety of excellent treatments to prevent attacks and relieve those that occur.

2.2 ASTHMA — MANAGEMENT

The management of asthma consists not only of drug treatment but also the holistic management of each asthmatic. It is important to know how asthma or its treatment affects each asthmatic; what are their hopes, aspirations, fears and expectations? How much do they know about asthma and its management? Is avoidance of triggers practicable and acceptable? Is the asthma, its effects and its treatment, being adequately monitored and assessed? Are the drugs used the best combinations of the best drugs in the best doses, given by the best method, and does the asthmatic know how and when to vary the dose, and call for help? Is each asthmatic as well-informed, confident and compliant as possible?

Education

What has happened

Until the 1960s asthma was poorly recognized and poorly treated. Both asthmatics and their carers, especially doctors, had low expectations of asthma management. Treatment was, by modern standards, crude and often had unpleasant side-effects. Asthma was regarded as a neurosis and some treatment, such as phenobarbitone, was directed primarily as sedation [1]. Thus a vicious cycle of poor expectations led to low compliance with treatment, which was largely unsatisfactory. This in turn led to poor symptom control, to disrupted lifestyles and to an increased stigma of having a poorly understood disease which barred the sufferer from participating in many aspects of everyday life. The stigma led on to low self-esteem of asthmatics and back to low expectations of successful management or improvement.

What can happen

This cycle can and should now be broken. The starting point of breaking the cycle should be an increase in the expectations of successful management of both asthmatics and their carers [2]. By simply stating the explicit aim that every asthmatic should lead a totally normal life unhampered by either their disease or its management, asthma care can be revolutionized. The aim can only be met by education, and by the education not only of asthmatics but also of their carers. The expectation of a normal life-style is more important than mere symptom control.

What should happen

Increasing the asthmatic's expectation of a normal life through the education of asthmatics, their parents, families, teachers, employers, and the public, should increase asthmatic compliance with management in order to improve symptom control, to achieve a less disrupted life-style, less stigmatization, higher self-esteem and even higher expectations [3]. Power over their disease can be given back to the asthmatic; the carer can help guide them on how best to achieve this.

Education for asthmatics should cover specific, detailed points formulated on an individual basis at practice level, by the various members of the primary health care team (general practitioner, practice nurse, community nurses, community physiotherapists, pharmacists and other professions allied to medicine). Education should also be for the professional carers to raise their awareness and their levels of expertise. Asking asthmatics the correct questions to establish how well-controlled they really are is a critical skill for healthcare professionals. On a wider level there should be education for all asthmatics and their relatives, and for raising the awareness of asthma for those who may have the disease but not the diagnosis. The latter is often at a national level, coordinated or initiated by such organizations as the National Asthma Campaign.

Sources of help

The National Asthma Campaign: a charity set up to promote education and research to improve the care of asthmatics. They produce an excellent range of videos, books and pamphlets for professionals and non-professionals. They will provide medical speakers for lectures or workshops for general practitioners and practice nurses. They have an information telephone line for patients.

The General Practitioners in Asthma Group consists of general practitioners and their practice nurses who have an interest in asthma. It initiates research and promotes the highest standards of asthma care.

The Asthma Training Centre: trains practice nurses to a high standard in providing asthma care.

The British Society for Allergy and Clinical Immunology: promotes research and initiatives in all aspects of allergies, including asthma.

Pharmaceutical companies: provide excellent materials for patients including leaflets, video and audio tapes. Some provide expert practical help in setting up, running and auditing asthma clinics and will sponsor educational meetings for doctors, nurses and pharmacists.

It is important not to try to teach too much too soon. Asthmatics are only human, and like us all, can only remember so much at a time. It will usually take several consultations before most asthmatics can assimilate all the knowledge they need. It is also important to try to listen to the asthmatic. Each will have their own fears, hopes, misinformed or ignorant opinion. Asthmatics should be encouraged to tell their professional carers how they feel and how they cope. This knowledge can be used to maximize the care provided for that individual, and for all asthmatics. Education is really a two-way process.

Assessment and monitoring

The severity of asthma is graded by the symptoms, by the drugs required to control it and by objective measurements. All three parameters are important. Not all asthmatics are equally accurate in assessing the changing severity of their disease as measured objectively. In all but the most mild and stable asthmatics, relying only on symptoms to assess severity, and therefore treatment, is unsatisfactory.

Peak flow meter assessment

Objective assessment is therefore necessary in most asthmatics. The easiest and cheapest method is to use a mini peak flow meter. These are comparatively cheap, can be prescribed on the NHS in the UK and are fairly consistent. It is sensible for general practitioners to prescribe the same meter that they use in their surgeries. It is also important to appreciate that different makes of meter are not entirely compatible and changes in peak flow are best assessed when the same meter is used consistently by the same patient. Prescribers and dispensers should try to be as precise as possible. The most commonly used meters last for about three years. Peak flow readings should be taken on waking and at about 5 pm before any bronchodilator is taken. The best of three readings, preferably taken standing up, should be recorded. Every asthmatic should know their best ever or predicted levels.

Symptom assessment

Patients may assess any changes in the severity of their asthma by symptoms, increased drug use and peak flow readings. The following indicate deterioration.

Symptoms: the development of night-time symptoms, especially if they wake the asthmatic; decreased exercise tolerance; day time cough; day time wheeze.

Drug use: increased bronchodilator use, especially serious if the relieving effect lasts for an increasingly short time, or appears increasingly less effective.

Peak flow readings: a fall in readings to less than 80% of best ever or expected readings or an increase in diurnal variation; a slow steady decline in readings; peak flow readings which improve by progressively smaller amounts in response to relieving treatment.

When to monitor the peak flow

One of the best ways of predicting and monitoring any deterioration of asthma is by measuring the peak flow. It is unrealistic to expect every asthmatic to measure their peak flow twice a day. However, those with severe asthma should do so, as should all asthmatics who have been newly diagnosed, had a recent increase or decrease in chronic maintenance therapy, who have had a recent acute exacerbation, those with a cold or other infection, before and during any times of predictably increased trigger exposure, or if they have any increase in symptoms or relieving drug use.

Peak flow management plans

All patients whose asthma is moderately severe or severe, whose asthma is at all unstable, or who are prone to sudden acute changes should have a peak flow management plan [4]. This relates the level of treatment to be taken for a given peak flow reading [5,6]. At 80–100% of best ever values, the usual maintenance treatment should be continued. At 60–80%, relieving treatment should be increased, usually vigorously; preventative treatment may also be increased and in all cases the asthma must be carefully monitored. Further peak flow decline should result in seeking medical help rapidly, or immediately if the peak flow is less than 60% normal. The peak flow management plan should be agreed by the asthmatic and the general practitioner or nurse. It should be written down in a way that both parties understand, with clear instructions on what to do and when, and when to call for help. Both parties should have copies of the plan. Each plan should be reviewed by both parties at least annually and after each exacerbation, especially if such an exacerbation resulted in severe symptoms and emergency treatment or admission (i.e. the plan failed). If treatment has been increased and the asthmatic has improved, it is usual to continue the increased treatments for as long as it took the asthmatic to return to usual peak flow levels before reducing back to maintenance levels. Examples of peak flow management are shown in Figures 2.2 and 2.3.

It may be helpful to give asthmatics peak flow charts on which the peak flow readings can be plotted. Horizontal lines corresponding to action levels can be drawn, so that if the peak flow falls below an agreed limit, the asthmatic knows what to do. A similar system can be used by sticking coloured tape on the peak flow meter to correspond to agreed levels. Again, crossing from the 'normal' zone to the 'danger zone' will trigger an increase in relieving (and maybe in preventative) treatment.

Peak Flow Management Plan

Your expected PF is [   ]

If your peak flow is:
a) above _____ , continue your usual treatment as prescribed.
b) between _____ and _____ , increase your _____ _____ to _____ x a day.
and/or, increase your _____ _____ to _____ x a day.
and/or start _____ _____ at _____ x a day.
and start _____ _____ at _____ x a day.

c) between _____ and _____ see your GP and treat as in (b).
d) less than 150 (75 in children) contact your doctor immediately and treat as in (b).

If you have increased your treatment or started a new drug, continue until your PF is over _____ (a). Stay at these doses for the same number of days it took you to get your PF back to normal.

If your PF does not increase in spite of these measures, contact your doctor at once.

If your PF drops as soon as you decrease or stop the extra treatment, see your doctor as soon as practicable.

(Note: a): 80 – 100% expected or best ever
b): 60 – 70% of expected or best ever
c): < 60% of expected or best ever).

Fig. 2.2 An example of peak flow management plan.

Avoidance and control of triggers

Most advances in the treatment of asthma have concentrated on suppressing the effects of asthma rather than eliminating the cause. This is because it is really much easier to treat the asthma with preventative or relieving drugs, which are increasingly sophisticated and relatively free of side-effects, especially if taken by inhalation. Eliminating the causes of asthma is difficult. Few asthmatics have only one or two known causes, and even if they are known, it is often nearly impossible to eliminate exposure to them.

Trigger avoidance

Common triggers of asthma are ubiquitous and some are impossible to avoid. Initially it is important to listen to what an asthmatic may think are important triggers for them, and to discuss possible avoidance with them. It is important to stress that total avoidance and control is nearly impossible and that it is often easier to treat the effects rather than radically altering one's life-style. The degree of

MANAGING YOUR OWN ASTHMA.

This plan is to help you control your asthma.

The plan involves the use of these medicines:

Zone One: ....
....

Zone Two: ....

Zone Three: ....

The plan depends to a large extent on your readings of peak flow.

You should measure and record your peak flow ....
....
.... when measured

Your target peak flow is ....
....

ZONE ONE:

Your asthma is under control if your peak flow is between ....
and .... and sleep is not disturbed and you are doing most of
your normal activities.

If your peak flow is in Zone One you should continue to take your
regular daily medicines which are:

1) .... taken in a dose of ....
.................................and

2) .... taken in a dose of ....

You should also take your .... to relieve
any coughing, wheezing, breathlessness or chest tightness.

ZONE TWO — CAUTION.

If your peak flow is between .... and .... or
you have chest tightness, wheeze or shortness of breath, then your
asthma is not well controlled.

If the peak flow has fallen into Zone Two quickly and the
symptoms developed suddenly, then TAKE .... doses of
your .... If that does not reduce your symptoms and
return your peak flow to Zone One within twenty minutes, or if
the Peak Flow fell to Zone Two more slowly (eg after a cold)
START oral Prednisolone (Steroid tablets) ...... mg (..... tablets)
daily and continue this dose until your target peak flow is reached.
You should then reduce by ...... mg (..... tablets) a day until you
reach
During this time you MUST continue to take your regular Zone One
treatment and make regular readings of Peak Flow. You should
inform your Doctor as soon as convenient after starting the course
of steroid tablets.

ZONE THREE — MEDICAL ALERT.

If your peak flow is below .... then immediate treatment is
needed. You should:

1) Take .... of .... and,
2) Take .... mg (................. tablets) of Prednisolone, and,
3) Call your Doctor/Ring for an Ambulance and/or,
4) ....

Do not be afraid of causing a fuss — your Doctor will want you to be
seen promptly so that treatment can be added to get you well again.

Fig. 2.3 Peak flow management plan for adults (National Asthma Campaign).

shifts in life-style will vary with the severity of the symptoms and personality of the asthmatic [7]. It is important that parents are not made to feel responsible for their child's asthma and that any changes they make must be as a result of full and frank discussion with the asthmatic patient rather than as a result of emotional reaction. The following are common triggers; the advice that follows is for those affected by that allergen.

House dust mite: ubiquitous especially in modern, centrally heated homes with insulation, double glazing and fitted carpets. Exposure can be reduced only with some difficulty. The full recipe is removal of all bedroom carpets, removal of all animal fibres, use of allergen non-permeable mattress covers, washing the curtains every 6 months and the bedding every week in a hot wash, keeping bedroom windows open and use of ascaricidal sprays. If all the above measures are assiduously applied, the house dust mite concentration can be reduced by up to 10 000 times, but it is unclear if this results in consistent clinical benefit [7]. It is perhaps easier to keep taking the medications for most patients.

Animals: the allergen is usually in their urine, saliva or dander. All pets should be completely banned from the bedrooms. Caged birds or mammals may be a hidden precipitant at school. Washing the cat weekly is helpful. Removal of any caged bird or animal from bedrooms and living rooms is advisable.

Occupational: once an asthmatic has been sensitized, subsequent exposure to even very low levels of sensitizer can trigger symptoms. A large number of substances have been implicated. It can often be impossible for a worker to continue in their employment without exposure to the trigger for their asthma. Whether to treat or change jobs needs discussing with each individual.

Food: dietary manipulation rarely modifies asthma. Occasionally an asthmatic will be sensitive to sulphites, a preservative used in beer, wine, dried fruit and processed potatoes.

Air pollution: exposure to smoke, sprays and polishes at home should be kept to a minimum. It is difficult for an individual to do much about air pollution.

Tobacco smoke: no asthmatic should smoke. No asthmatic should be exposed to others' smoke—especially children [8,9].

Drugs: aspirin, especially, and other non-steroidal anti-inflammatory drugs can worsen symptoms in certain asthmatics. Particular care should be taken with the administration of beta-blockers, even as eye drops, as such drugs commonly exacerbate or precipitate asthma.

Exercise: for the majority of people normal recreational exercise is enjoyable. It is usually best to use drug treatment to allow appropriate exercise than reduce the need for drugs by forced inactivity and prohibiting what should be an essential part of life.

Upper respiratory tract infections: these are nearly always viral and are one of the most common triggers cited by asthmatics. At the first sign of such infection it is important to increase the asthma therapy and to monitor the peak flow and symptoms [10]. It is sensible for those with more severe or unstable asthma to try to avoid contact, if possible, with other people suffering from heavy colds, influenza or other viral illnesses.

Desensitization was a popular therapy in the UK until the mid 1980s, when the resulting mortality rate was considered unacceptable. It is still used in North America and the rest of Europe. The efficacy of most desensitizing agents for asthma (as opposed to anaphylaxis) is still doubtful. Desensitization should only be undertaken where full resuscitation can be safely carried out and all patients can be monitored for at least 2 hours after each treatment.

Other non-drug therapies: ionizers, hypnotherapy, acupuncture, homeopathy and other treatments may help certain asthmatics but there is insufficient evidence to advocate any of these therapies more widely.

Primary avoidance: finally, an infant who does not want to develop asthma should choose:
non-atopic parents;
to be a girl;
a mother who does not smoke in pregnancy but does breast feed;
a household where no one smokes;
parents who are meticulous cleaners and who hate dust mites;
not to be born prematurely;
not to be born in the spring!

Medication

Of all the common chronic conditions managed mainly in the community, none has the range, specificity, safety profile and quality of medications available to treat it as asthma has.

Treatments

The range of treatments available and the different ways of using them are confusing to doctor and patient alike.

There are six main categories.

1 Beta-2 agonists.
2 Theophyllines.
3 Anticholinergics.
4 Corticosteroids.
5 Disodium cromoglycate and nedocromil.
6 Long acting beta-2 agonists.

Beta-2 agonists

Action: bronchodilators which stimulate the beta-2 adrenergic receptors in the bronchial smooth muscle causing relaxation of the muscle; they also enhance mucociliary clearance and decrease vascular permeability.

Uses: short-acting beta-2 agonists are the treatment of choice for the relief of exacerbations of asthma and may be of value in the prophylaxis of exercise-induced asthma. All asthmatics should have a short-acting beta-2 agonist, preferably given by inhalation. Ideally none would ever need it except as described above.

Short-acting beta-2 agonists may be the only treatment needed for mild asthma [11]. However, increasing evidence that there may be an inflammatory element even in mild asthma means that preventative treatment is increasingly advocated in all but the mildest cases.

It has been suggested that regular, frequent use of beta-2 agonists as the only treatment may mask the underlying decline in lung-function that may occur in some asthmatics not treated with preventative agents [12].

Routes: can be given by inhalation using aerosols or dry powder devices, or nebulizer, or by tablets, syrup, or injection.

Side-effects:
Inhaled: very few. Some susceptible individuals may experience tremor, tachycardia, or headache.
Oral: usually mild and transient. Palpitations, tremor and tachycardia are the most common; hypokalaemia, cramp and headaches

may occur. Use with caution in thyrotoxicosis, uncompensated cardiac failure and cardiomyopathies.

Cost:

Inhaled: very cheap especially if given by metered-dose aerosol. Other devices may be more expensive but may provide more reliable drug delivery.

Oral: very cheap. Long-acting preparations are a little more expensive.

Examples and choices: the inhaled route is to be preferred if at all possible. There is little to choose between the main preparations salbutamol and terbutaline, and the choice of inhaler device is probably more important. Oral preparations are sometimes used for therapeutic trials—syrups in small children, longer-acting tablets in the elderly. However, if more regular therapy is then initiated it is preferable to switch to an inhaled route.

Theophyllines

Action: the precise mechanism is unclear. They are undoubtedly bronchodilators with some central stimulant action.

Uses: their narrow therapeutic range and the risk of adverse effects limits their usefulness. Long-acting formulations are effective for night symptom suppression. Often given for childhood asthma, they are more widely used in North America than in the UK, where they are usually regarded as third-line agents.

Routes: can be given parenterally to terminate severe acute asthma, preferably under ECG control. Can be given orally, rectally or parenterally. The latter two routes are not recommended for routine use. Their main disadvantage is that they cannot be given by inhalation.

Side-effects: nausea, vomiting, tachycardia, arrhythmias, insomnia, seizures and sudden death. The effects are less common at therapeutic doses, for which monitoring of blood levels is recommended. Some advocate using technically sub-therapeutic doses and continuing them if there is a good clinical response. Blood levels may be affected by other illnesses, pregnancy, other drugs, heart failure, liver disease and diet.

Cost: fairly cheap. The sustained-release preparations are a little more expensive.

Examples and choices: sustained-release preparations are better for the relief of nocturnal symptoms. Titrate the dose against efficacy, up to the manufacturer's recommended dose, and monitor blood levels. The theophylline bioavailability from different preparations is not equivalent so do not swap brands unnecessarily.

Anticholinergics

Action: bronchodilators which block post-ganglionic vagal pathways, so reducing vagally-induced bronchoconstriction; less potent and act more slowly than beta-agonists.

Uses: as an alternative if an asthmatic is very sensitive to beta-agonists. May have an additive effect when nebulized together with a beta-agonist in acute asthma [15]. May be of use in very young infants and in mixed, partially reversible obstructive airways disease in late middle to old age.

Routes: inhalation only. Side-effects are unacceptable with oral preparations. By inhalers or nebulization.

Side-effects: rare. Avoid with glaucoma. Bad taste, dry mouth, blurred vision, urinary problems.

Costs: fairly cheap.

Examples and choices: ipratropium is shorter-acting but useful when nebulized. Oxitropium is more expensive but slightly longer-acting.

Corticosteroids

Action: preventative; potent anti-inflammatory. Act by a variety of cellular, local hormonal and chemical pathways. They reduce mucus viscosity and increase beta-receptor responsiveness.

Uses:
Inhaled: in chronic asthma they are used in low doses for the management of mild to moderate asthma and at higher doses (more than $800\,\mu g$/day in adults) for more severe asthma. They control the underlying inflammation and thereby reduce the severity and frequency of acute attacks. The dose may be temporarily increased to give added protection at times of increased risk, such as with a cold.

It is hoped that chronic use may prevent the long-term damage to the lungs that might otherwise occur [16]. Inhaled steroids are the drug of choice for the good control of most asthma [17].
Oral: in acute asthma, their early administration prevents progression of the exacerbation and reduces the need for hospitalization, and reduces morbidity. Thus they are very useful in high doses to treat severe acute exacerbations. In chronic asthma they may

need to be used long-term at low doses for the management of very severe asthma.

Routes: inhalation: by aerosol, powder or nebulizer. Oral; intravenous.

Side-effects:

Inhaled steroids: oral thrush, deepening or hoarseness of the voice. Systemic absorption is probably of minimal importance if the total daily dose is 800 μg or less, even in children. Higher doses should usually be taken through a large volume spacer to attempt to minimize oral absorption [18]. The mouth should be rinsed after every dose of inhaled steroids to avoid local oral problems. The effects of inhaled steroids on childrens' growth has been extensively studied [19,20]. Undoubtedly inhaled steroids are preferable to oral steroids in allowing normal growth. There is no clear evidence of long-term growth suppression at doses less than 800 μg a day of beclomethasone or budesonide for up to 8 years. Even in pre-school children, doses of less than 400 μg a day did not result in growth suppression. At doses higher than this the risk:benefit ratio must be re-evaluated; however, asthma kills; short stature if it occurs does not. Indeed poorly controlled asthma can itself lead to growth retardation [19]. The total annual dose of steroid absorbed from regularly inhaled doses is likely to be less than that of two or three courses of oral steroid use. Inhaled steroids not only lead to better control of asthma symptoms but to decreased frequency and severity of exacerbations and subsequent need for courses of oral steroids.

Fluticasone propionate is a recently introduced inhaled steroid and is an advance on current inhaled steroid therapy. It appears to possess a more potent anti-inflammatory action than other currently available steroids, coupled with negligible oral systemic bioavailability [21]. Oral absorption is very low (< 1%) and any absorbed drug is rapidly and completely metabolized to an inert metabolite by the liver [22]. The risk of any systemic side-effects or effect on adrenal suppression may therefore be reduced. It is therefore potentially valuable for patients on long-term higher-dose steroids and for children (currently licensed for 4-year-old or older).

Oral steroids:

Short-term: increased appetite; bad dreams, euphoria. There is no evidence even in children of adrenal suppression if four or fewer courses a year are given, each of less than 21 days [19].

Long-term: adrenal suppression, raised blood sugar, psychiatric problems, weight gain, thin skin, osteoporosis, redistribution of fat.

Note: fatal varicella (chickenpox) can occur in patients susceptible to it, who are on oral steroids, even short-term [23]. If such a patient is exposed, stop the steroid if feasible and give zoster immunoglobulin and oral acyclovir if varicella develops.

Costs: cheap. If given by some of the non-metered dose aerosol devices, they are more expensive, especially at high doses, but may provide more reliable drug delivery.

Examples and choices: there is little to choose between the two inhaled steroids budesonide and beclomethasone dipropionate. The choice of device is probably of more importance than the choice of steroid. Fluticasone propionate may be the treatment of choice in patients requiring higher doses of inhaled steroids, particularly those who are still growing.

Disodium cromoglycate and nedocromil sodium

Action: preventative; anti-inflammatory, mainly at a cellular level. Nedocromil produces some reduction in airway responsiveness. No bronchodilator action [24].

Uses: only as preventative therapies. Prophylaxis against exercise-induced symptoms.

Routes: by inhalation: aerosol (both), dry powder (cromoglycate only), nebulization (cromoglycate only).

Side effects: coughing on inhalation.

Costs: both relatively expensive, nedocromil especially so.

Examples and choices: cromoglycate is useful in children, generally less so in adults, but there is insufficient evidence to predict accurately which patients will benefit. A 6 week trial is required to determine efficacy. Nedocromil can as yet only be promoted for adults. Either drug may be useful when inhaled steroids cannot or will not be tolerated. The main disadvantage is that they must be taken three or four times daily to be effective.

Long-acting beta-agonists

Action: long-acting bronchodilators, either intrinsically (salmeterol xinafoate, bambuterol) or as a result of formulation (controlled-release salbutamol and terbutaline).

Uses: when symptom control is still poor despite use of inhaled anti-inflammatory agents, or as an alternative to increasing the dose of inhaled steroids in those having problems with this treatment, or where night-time symptoms are particulary prominent but the control of the asthma is otherwise satisfactory. Long-acting beta-agonists are given for their protective effect against bronchospasm and should not be used for immediate relief of acute wheeze, for which short-acting inhaled beta-agonists are more effective.

Routes: by inhalation (aerosol or powder); oral.

Side-effects: When given by inhalation they are relatively free of side-effects and of low potential toxicity compared with long-acting oral beta-agonists and theophyllines. Tremor, palpitations, and headache may occur in some patients.

Costs: relatively expensive.

Examples and choices: salmeterol xinafoate (inhaled). Slow release salbutamol tablets, bambuterol (oral).

Table 2.1 shows details of the drugs most often used.

The devices

Note: an inhaler is any device which delivers a drug by inhalation. 'Inhalers' is a collective term for metered-dose aerosols, Rotahalers, Diskhalers, Volumatics, Nebuhalers, nebulizers, Autohalers, Spinhalers and Turbohalers.* A metered-dose aerosol is a specific propellant-driven device.

In treating asthma, care in explaining and demonstrating inhaler technique may be of more importance than choice of drugs in a particular category.

> The correct choice of device and proper teaching of its use can be fundamental in determining the level of success in treating asthma.

Metered-dose aerosol: the 'universal' inhaler, often known simply as the aerosol inhaler or metered-dose inhaler (MDI). Propellant driven, currently contains chlorofluorocarbons (CFCs). Portable,

*Rotahaler, Diskhaler and Volumatic are trademarks of Allen and Hanburys Limited; Turbohaler and Nebuhaler are trademarks of Astra Pharmaceuticals; Spinhaler and Fisonair are trademarks of Fisons; Autohaler is a trademark of 3M.

Table 2.1 Drugs commonly used for asthma [41, 42]

Class	Proper name
Beta agonists	*short-acting* Salbutamol Terbutaline Bambuterol Fenoterol Orciprenaline Pirbuterol Reproterol Rimiterol Tulobuterol *long-acting* Salmeterol xinafoate
Theophylline derivatives	Aminophylline Theophylline Choline theophyllate
Anticholinergics	Ipratropium bromide Oxitropium bromide
Anti-inflammatories	Disodium cromoglycate Nedocromil
Corticosteroids	Beclomethasone dipropionate Budesonide Fluticasone propionate Prednisolone
Compound preparations	Fenoterol/Ipratropium Salbutamol/Beclomethasone dipropionate

Principles: it is best to use the inhaled route if possible and it is best to select an inhaler which the asthmatic can efficiently use, which best delivers an effective dose of drug to the lungs, and which allows dose monitoring to occur.

easy for some to use, no preparation except shaking, quick, unobtrusive. Very useful when the technique can be properly learnt and is regularly checked. Nearly all inhaled drugs are available as MDIs even if they come as other inhalers as well. These are the cheapest devices. Their main disadvantage is that many asthmatics cannot and do not use them properly and so do not derive the full benefit from the drug which has been imperfectly delivered.

This can potentially be overcome by using a spacer device; the MDI is actuated into the spacer, which acts as a reservoir from which the drug is inhaled without the need to co-ordinate actuation of the MDI with inspiration. Both small and large-volume types are available. The small-volume spacer is readily portable; large-volume devices are unwieldy and not readily portable. Very easy to use. Cheap, and as they are used with aerosols, a cheaper way of giving effective treatment if many preparations or for when high doses are needed [25]. When used with high-dose steroids the risk of oral candidiasis and systemic effects occurring is reduced. Very useful for the elderly, who cannot co-ordinate their breathing to use metered-dose aerosols, or use their fingers to use dry powder devices. Very useful for small children, even babies, when used in conjunction with a face mask whilst holding the device vertically [26]. If the large-volume spacer is held vertically the valve falls open and minimal inspiratory flow is needed for the inhalation of the drug into the lungs. Every child given inhaled steroids from a metered-dose inhaler should use a large-volume spacer to increase the fraction of drug delivered to the lung and decrease the fraction swallowed [26]. In an emergency, it can be used as a substitute for a nebulizer (if none is available) if sufficient doses are released into the chamber. The Nebuhaler can be used with budesonide and terbutaline aerosols. The Volumatic can be used with salbutamol, beclomethasone dipropionate, salbutamol and beclomethasone combination and salmeterol xinafoate aerosols. The Fisonair is available for use with sodium cromoglycate but the inhaler port is shaped to fit most aerosols. An ingenious expedient for emergency use in infants is to use a polystyrene cup. Inset the mouth of an MDI through the bottom of the cup. Actuation of the aerosol with the top of the cup covering the infant's mouth and nose means that the cup acts as a small-volume spacer device. Use of a large-volume spacer, held vertically, with a soft plastic mask is preferable and more reliable.

Rotahaler: dry powder, breath-operated. Easy to use, portable, single dose. Lactose taste confirms that the dose has been taken. Used with salbutamol and beclomethasone dipropionate. Fairly cheap.

Diskhaler: dry powder, breath-operated. Very easy to use, multiple doses, portable. Each dose is individually blister-sealed and so protected from moisture. Lactose taste confirms dose has been taken. Dose monitoring (doses used and doses left) is easy due to numbered blisters. Popular with school children and their parents. Requires less inspiratory effort than Rotahalers. Used for salbutamol, beclomethasone dipropionate, salmeterol xinafoate and fluticasone propionate. Relatively expensive.

Turbohaler: dry powder, breath operated, multiple doses. Very easy to use. No taste indicator. Cannot monitor the doses used but has a device to warn when nearly empty. Can be used by small children (although the dose delivery may be unreliable in children under

5), and those with poor eyesight or co-ordination. Used for terbuta-line and budesonide. Relatively expensive.

Autohalers: breath-activated metered-dose aerosol. Easy to use but no monitoring or indication when nearly empty. Makes a loud click which may be disconcerting. Used for salbutamol and beclometha-sone. Relatively expensive.

Spinhaler: breath operated dry powder. Fiddly but easy to actually inhale. Unique to cromoglycate.

Nebulizers: gas-driven droplets. For emergency treatment of severe exacerbations or regular treatment in infants unable to use a large-volume spacer and mask; in adults unable to obtain control despite correctly complying with full anti-inflammatory therapy and adequate inhaler technique. If given in emergency, use oxygen to drive the nebulizer if possible. Delivers a large dose of the drug. Time-consuming. Excellent for emergency use for which it should be reserved with rare exceptions. Use with salbutamol, terbutaline, beclomethasone, budesonide, ipratropium, cromoglycate. Nebulizers require supervision and regular cleaning and maintenance.

Regular nebulized bronchodilators should only be given when other methods of drug administration have been tried or rejected, where there is good compliance with anti-inflammatory treatments, and increased bronchodilatation, without unacceptable side-effects, can be shown. A 3-week home trial with peak flow monitoring is advised. Written and verbal instructions should be given to the asthmatic on the method, frequency of use, action to be taken if deterioration occurs and when to attend for follow-up. Supervision should usually be by a trained asthma nurse or physiotherapist or at an asthma clinic.

Supervision should include prescription monitoring, peak flow evaluation, and servicing of the compressor bi-annually.

Choice of device

The underlying principle of all devices is to deliver an effective dose of the drug directly to the lungs, so that only a low dose is needed but one which achieves a high concentration where it is needed (in the bronchi) and a low concentration where it is not (in the rest of the body).

It is preferable to find a delivery system that delivers both relieving and preventative drugs. It is best to show the asthmatic all the devices and let them try them out. As optimal drug delivery is the main criterion when choosing a device, the prescriber should

Table 2.2 Suggested devices for use by asthmatic children at different ages

Age (years)	Inhalation delivery system	Bronchodilator treatment	Preventative treatment
< 2	Nebulizer Face mask and large-volume spacer or proximal half of spacer without mask	Salbutamol Terbutaline Ipratropium	Cromoglycate Beclomethasone dipropionate Budesonide
2–4	Metered-dose aerosol with large-volume spacer Nebulizer for emergencies	Salbutamol Terbutaline Ipratropium	Cromoglycate Beclomethasone dipropionate Budesonide
4–8	Dry powder devices Metered-dose aerosol with large-volume spacer for emergencies	Salbutamol Terbutaline	Cromoglycate Beclomethasone dipropionate Budesonide Fluticasone propionate
> 8	Dry powder devices Metered-dose inhalers Autohalers	Salbutamol Terbutaline	Cromoglycate Beclomethasone dipropionate Budesonide Fluticasone propionate

recommend the device most appropriate for each patient. The professional carer must instruct the patient on how to use the inhaler, ensure that it is being used correctly, and periodically check that it is still being used correctly—at least annually, but ideally at each visit to the surgery. Pharmacists can check those getting repeat prescriptions whenever a new device is dispensed.

In children particular care must be taken in choosing delivery systems. It is especially important to ensure that the child has sufficient inspiratory flow to obtain an adequate dose of the drug in the bronchi. Suggested devices for different ages are shown in Table 2.2 [27].

Guidelines for inhaler use

Metered-dose aerosols: sit upright, shake the aerosol to ensure that it is not empty and to mix its contents. Hold the head and the inhaler upright. Exhale completely. Place the mouthpiece in the mouth and close the lips firmly around it. Breathe in smoothly and slowly. As you begin to breath in actuate the inhaler by depressing the inhaler top to release the spray. Carry on breathing in one smooth breath, drawing the spray deep into the lungs. When you have fully inhaled, hold your breath for 10 seconds, or as long as is comfortable, then exhale. If a second does is to be taken, wait approximately half a minute to allow your breathing to return to normal. Once your breathing is back to a normal pattern (usually immediately) repeat the process if a second dose is to be taken.

Large-volume spacers: as above, shake the aerosol canister before inserting into the casing. Hold the spacer horizontally. Depress the aerosol top the required number of times according to the dose, no more than two actuations at once and preferably one at a time, repeating the process if necessary if the dose is higher than two puffs. Exhale fully, place the mouthpiece in the mouth, make a good seal with the lips. Inhale slowly, hold breath for 5 seconds, then exhale through the mouthpiece. Continue for two or three breaths. In small infants use a soft, inverted face mask for the Nebuhaler or a similar mask for the Volumatic. Hold the spacer vertically with the mouthpiece at the lower end after actuation of the aerosol or aerosols [28].

Dry-powder and breath-operated devices: exhale fully, place the mouth firmly around the mouthpiece and inhale deeply and smoothly. Hold the breath for at least 10 seconds, remove the device from the mouth, exhale. Different devices may require different procedures to prime the device prior to inhalation. Most dry powder devices require an inspiratory flow-rate of 30–60 l/min in order to deliver the dose of drug satisfactorily to the lungs so patients should be instructed to inhale briskly and deeply.

The management plans for chronic persistent asthma

The aim is to use the minimum dose of drugs that will achieve good control of the asthma. The criteria of good control are:
no or minimal day-time and night symptoms;
no or minimal exacerbations;
no or minimal need for relieving treatment;
good exercise tolerance;
no or minimal diurnal peak flow variability (less than 20%);
peak flow rates of at least 80% predicted or best ever;
no or minimal adverse effects of treatment.

The stepwise approach to asthma is a description of the levels of treatment required to achieve good asthma control. If control from treatment at a particular step is not adequate, based on the criteria above, treatment must be increased to the next level or step. Patients should start at the step most appropriate for the initial severity of their condition. As asthma is a chronic inflammatory condition, most patients will need to receive anti-inflammatory drugs. All should receive a short-acting bronchodilator for relief of symptoms should they occur.

A rescue course of oral steroids may be needed at any time and at any step.

The following is based on the revised *BTS Guidelines* of 1993 devised by the British Thoracic Society, Research Unit of the Royal College of Physicians of London, King's Fund Centre, the National Asthma Campaign, the Royal College of General Practitioners, the General Practitioners in Asthma Group, the British Association of Accident and Emergency Medicine and the British Paediatric Respiratory group and on the revised statement from the Paediatric Asthma Consensus Group of 1992 [27,29].

The steps: adults
Step 1: occasional use of relief bronchodilators

Short-acting beta-agonists should be used to relieve symptoms as required rather than regularly. They can also be used before exercise. The inhaled route should be used if at all possible. If these drugs are needed more than once a day on average, step up treatment.

Step 2: regular inhaled anti-inflammatory agents

Short-acting beta-agonists, preferably inhaled, *plus* inhaled beclomethasone dipropionate or budesonide 100–400 μg twice daily or fluticasone propionate 100–200 μg twice daily. Cromoglycate or nedocromil sodium can be used as alternatives.

Anti-inflammatory agents should be started if short-acting beta agonists are needed more than once a day or in the presence of night time symptoms. To gain initial control a higher dose of steroid may be needed, but the dose should be minimized to maintain control. Some patients benefit from doubling the dose of inhaled steroid to cover a respiratory infection.

If cromoglycate or nedocromil sodium is begun and control is not achieved despite full doses after 4–6 weeks, change to inhaled steroids before moving to Step 3.

Step 3: high-dose regular inhaled steroids

Short-acting beta-agonist, preferably inhaled, *plus* inhaled beclomethasone dipropionate or budesonide 800–2000 μg daily preferably via a large-volume spacer or fluticasone propionate 400–1000 μg daily.

A few patients who experience problems with high-dose inhaled steroids may achieve good control using inhaled long-acting beta-agonists or even sustained-release theophyllines in addition to their Step 2 therapy. Cromoglycate or nedocromil sodium can be tried.

If night time symptoms are particularly prominent and the asthma is otherwise well controlled, inhaled long-acting beta-agonists should be considered (or oral long-acting beta-agonists or sustained release theophyllines if the inhaled route is impossible) in addition to the Step 2 therapy. Salmeterol has the advantage of being an inhaled preparation, which is relatively free from side-effects and interactions with other drugs.

Step 4: high-dose inhaled steroids and regular broncho- dilators

Step 3 therapy *plus* a sequential therapeutic trial of one or more of: inhaled long-acting beta-agonists; inhaled ipratropium or oxitropium; high-dose inhaled short-acting beta-agonists; oral long-acting beta-agonists; oral sustained-release theophyllines; cromoglycate or nedocromil sodium.

High doses of inhaled short-acting bronchodilators should only be considered if there has been an inadequate response to standard doses. Short-acting beta-agonists and anticholinergic drugs can be given via a nebulizer.

Step 5: addition of regular oral steroids

Step 4 therapy *plus* regular oral steroids in a single daily dose.

Step up

When control cannot be maintained at the current step. Before stepping up always check and adjust if necessary: compliance; inhaler technique; education. If the symptoms are severe or the peak flow less than 50% predicted or best ever, give a short course of oral steroids and move up a step.

Step down

When control has been well maintained for at least 3 months, consider stepping down. Stepping down from Steps 4 or 5 may be considered earlier. Peak flow monitoring should be continued during all reductions of therapy. Each asthmatic must know how to recognize deterioration and what to do about it.

Rescue courses or oral steroids: may be needed to control exacerbations at any step. Indications may include: progressive, daily worsening of symptoms and/or peak flow; peak flow less than 60% of best ever;

sleep disturbed by asthma;
morning symptoms persisting until noon;
diminishing response to inhaled bronchodilators;
need for emergency nebulizations.

Steroids should be given in full doses (30–60 mg daily) and continued for at least 2 days after control is re-established.

The steps: children
Step 1: occasional use of relief bronchodilators

As for adults. Use inhaled therapy wherever possible.

Step 2: regular inhaled anti-inflammatory agents

Intermittent inhaled short-acting beta-agonists as required *plus* cromoglycate.

Use cromoglycate as powder, 20 μg three times a day, or via metered-dose inhaler and large-volume spacer, 10 μg three times a day. If good control is not reached after 4–6 weeks, step up.

Step 3: inhaled steroids

Inhaled short-acting beta-agonists as required *plus* beclomethasone dipropionate, fluticasone propionate or budesonide.

It may be necessary to start at a higher dose or to give a short course of oral steroids to achieve stabilization. Adjust the dose according to symptoms and peak flow readings after 1 month. If using a metered-dose inhaler, use a large-volume spacer. Fluticasone is currently licensed for children aged 4 years and over.

Step 4: high-dose inhaled steroids or inhaled long-acting beta-agonists

Inhaled short-acting beta-agonists as required *plus* beclomethasone dipropionate, fluticasone propionate or budesonide daily via a large-volume spacer or dry-powder device up to recommended doses; consider adding regular twice daily inhaled long-acting beta-agonists.

Inhaled long-acting beta-agonists are effective for up to 12 hours per dose and also are an effective prophylaxis against exercise induced asthma.

Step 5(a): high-dose inhaled steroids and bronchodilators

Step 4 therapy *plus* slow-release theophyllines or nebulized beta-agonists.

Step 5(b): regular oral steroids

Step 5(a) therapy *plus* alternate-day low-dose oral steroids.

Theophyllines have appreciable side-effects in up to one-third of all children. Sustained release beta-agonist tablets are equally effective but have fewer side-effects.

Step up

As for adults. Short courses of oral steroids may be tried before commencing the higher dose inhaled steroids for prolonged periods (Steps 3 to 4). Always check compliance, inhaler technique, appropriateness of each drug and inhaler device and education and knowledge of the child and parents.

Step down

Review more regularly than in adults especially at Steps 3–5. Monitor all reductions carefully, including peak flow readings if feasible. Stop regular anti-inflammatory drugs after 6–12 months of few or no symptoms.

There is no evidence that long-term inhaled steroids at doses of less than 400 μg a day are harmful. There is growing evidence of the safety of inhaled steroids at these doses used for up to 8 years [19,20]. The addition of regular, long-term inhaled steroids should be decided on after full informed discussion with the parents if compliance is to be achieved. The younger the child, the more severe the asthma should be before starting long-term inhaled steroids. Many prescribers and parents prefer to introduce inhaled steroids earlier than proposed in these guidelines, either to aid compliance or because the inhaled steroids are considered more effective for that individual.

Self management plans for deteriorating asthma

Models of management

Asthma is a chronic disease of variable severity. One of the aims of asthma management is to abolish acute exacerbations but this is not always possible. Another aim is that any exacerbations are promptly recognized and treated. Until comparatively recently the model was that the asthmatic waited until they felt worse; they then consulted their doctor who then modified their treatment. Problems with this model in practice were that asthmatics waited until they felt unwell before being able to alter their treatment, and then it needed a doctor to authorize the change. The asthmatic was not empowered to intervene in their own management. An additional problem was that asthmatics could only rely on symptom changes to trigger treatment changes: many asthmatics can have a considerable decline in lung function before becoming symptomatic. The asthmatic also had to wait for deterioration to occur before being able to relieve it instead of being in a position of being able to monitor the disease and its effects and instigate treatment changes early in the deterioration, so preventing further deterioration and a more prolonged and severe exacerbation.

The current model usually employed is to empower the asthmatic to alter their therapy in certain circumstances. This implies that the asthmatic is aware of worsening asthma by being able to:
recognize the symptoms;
realize the implication of increased need for relievers;
objectively measure the deterioration.

Recognizing deterioration

In other words there are three ways of recognizing deteriorating asthma and every asthmatic should be instructed and educated about each [30]. An increase in the symptoms of cough, wheeze, chest tightness and shortness of breath, especially at night, or a decrease in exercise tolerance, should alert the asthmatic to the need for increased medication and increased surveillance. If symptom control can be maintained but only by using more relieving drugs, especially if the drugs seem to work less well or for less time, then the asthma is deteriorating. Finally peak flow readings provide an excellent objective measurement of airways obstruction. A change in symptoms or need for relieving treatment should certainly be an indication for mild to moderate asthmatics to start twice daily peak flow reading until the levels are consistently normal again. It is probably unreasonable for these asthmatics to be measuring their peak flow twice daily continuously but they should certainly do so in the circumstances mentioned, as well as when treatment has been altered, they have a cold or other infection, or are going to be or have been exposed to a known trigger (such as staying in a house with pets). Asthmatics with moderate to severe asthma should measure their peak flow regularly all the time.

Recognition of deterioration is, then important. The asthmatic (or parent) then needs to know what to do, how to do it, and what to do if the exacerbation does or does not get better.

What to do if deteriorating

What to do: for a given peak flow reduction, the asthmatic needs to know how to increase the medication [27]. Certain falls in the peak flow rates are taken as significant: a fall to 80% of its predicted or best ever value and a fall to 60% of its predicted value [31]. At levels above 80% of predicted the asthmatic continues their chronic medication. At levels between 60% and 80%, they should either double the dose of their preventative therapy, or start, if not usually taking it. They should also take their reliever medication regularly every

4 hours or so and continue monitoring their peak flow. If it returns to that predicted, the asthmatic should stay on the higher levels of therapy for the same number of days it took to get there. If deterioration persists and peak flow falls to below 60% (or does not improve after a few days) then the asthmatic should seek help.

Some asthmatics may have oral steroids at home and these should be started while waiting to see the doctor or nurse if the peak flow has fallen to 60% predicted (75 l/min in children under 8 years old) emergency care should be sought, either from the general practitioner or, if not available, from the local accident and emergency department, if necessary by dialling 999. This advice is also recommended if any asthmatic has very severe symptoms which are not promptly relieved by the increased treatment.

The control of asthma

These asthma management plans give control to the asthmatic. This control can only be effectively used if the asthmatic has received sufficient education, training and monitoring, and is compliant with treatment and can use their inhalers correctly. The management plans need to be tailored for each asthmatic and to be negotiated and agreed by each asthmatic and their professional carers. The plans need to be written down and both parties should keep a copy. Each plan should be reviewed at least annually and after each exacerbation to see if it was as effective as possible. Most asthmatics should have a formal self-management plan, and most should be based on peak flow readings rather than only on symptoms. Even if an asthmatic does not have a self-management plan they must at least know how to recognize deterioration and when and how to call for help. Examples of self-management plans are included in Figures 2.2 and 2.3.

Temporary increases in treatment are also recommended to cover periods of increased risk of deterioration, such as colds or other infections [10], and also to cover periods of travel or being away from home. The higher levels of treatment should ideally be started before exposure and continued for 2 or 3 days after the exposure is over.

Oral steroids

Short-course oral steroid therapy should be in a dose of 2 mg/kg for children, and 30–60 mg daily for adults. The complete daily dose should be taken at one time, preferably in the mornings to avoid sleep disturbance. Oral steroids should be started at agreed points in the self-management plan. Some asthmatics who experience sudden severe exacerbations in response to certain triggers, such as colds or allergen exposure, may benefit from prompt oral steroid use before or as soon as possible after exposure. When taking oral steroids asthmatics should monitor their peak flow and continue on the steroids until the peak flow is consistently normal and then for at least a further 2 days. There is no need to diminish the dose gradually if courses last less than a month. The threshold for using oral steroids will vary with each asthmatic. Those whose exacerbations have previously been sudden or severe should take them at a very early stage, sometimes with only a 20% drop in peak flow or with the first symptoms of deterioration.

Problems associated with asthma

Exercise: this is a common trigger of asthma and in some asthmatics it is the only one. If exercise induces airways obstruction which reverses 30 to 45 minutes following physical activity, the condition is referred to as exercise-induced asthma (EIA). EIA is worse when breathing in cold air. EIA may be due to poor underlying asthma control and completion of a symptom diary with daily peak flows may be helpful in recognizing poorly controlled asthma. Better overall control, especially if anti-inflammatory drugs are used, will benefit EIA. Specific therapy is best given pre-exercise. Inhaled beta-agonists, especially the long-acting ones, combined with sufficient warming-up pre-exercise are the most effective prophylaxis although inhaled cromoglycate, nedocromil, steroids and anticholinergics have also proved effective. Exercise should not be prevented or curtailed in asthmatics. If EIA occurs, treatment is greatly preferable to curtailing exercise. One of the aims of asthma management is to allow every asthmatic to exercise appropriately.

Upper airways disease: asthma is often associated with rhinitis, sinusitis and nasal polyps [32]. Proper attention to and treatment of these conditions will facilitate effective asthma management.

The very young (0–2 years) present particular problems. The diagnosis rests almost entirely on the symptoms which may be variable. There are few controlled trials of treatments and devices; bronchodilator response may be variable but is often worthwhile. Inhaled therapy is preferable to oral. Nebulization at this age can produce initial paroxysmal bronchoconstriction so a large-volume spacer, held vertically with a soft face mask or using only its proximal half, with a metered dose aerosol bronchodilator is preferable.

Pregnancy: some asthmatic women will find pregnancy worsens their asthma, some that it improves it and some that it makes no difference

[33]. Anti-asthma medications are generally safe to use during pregnancy. Systemic corticosteroids given chronically have been associated with decreased birthweight of the baby; beta-agonists and theophyllines given near the time of birth may be associated with reversible jitteriness and tachycardia in the newborn infant. Ephedrine and brompheniramine may have adverse effects on the fetus and should be avoided [34]. Severe asthma, especially with hypoxia, undoubtedly does adversely affect the fetus. It is therefore advisable to continue appropriate preventative treatment throughout pregnancy and to treat vigorously any exacerbations. High-dose beta-agonists can inhibit uterine contractions but this is not clinically relevant if they are given by inhalation [34].

Other drugs: aspirin and to a lesser extent other non-steroidal anti-inflammatory drugs may precipitate asthma in adults. It is preferable for all adult asthmatics to avoid aspirin. Those with a history suggestive of aspirin-induced asthma should definitely always avoid it [35]. Challenging with aspirin should only take place in hospital when the asthma is in remission. There are no useful *in vitro* tests for this condition.

Gastro-oesophageal reflux: is associated with asthma as a concomitant condition. If suspected clinically the possibility should be investigated and appropriate treatment and advice instigated if necessary.

Respiratory infections: one of the most commonly cited triggers for asthma is upper respiratory tract infection (URTI) [36]. These are often unavoidable [37] but at the first symptoms or signs of such an infection, asthma therapy should be stepped up. Moderate or severe asthmatics should receive influenza vaccination each autumn.

Psychosocial factors: asthma may cause anxiety or depression in sufferers and their carers. Asthma and psychological or psychiatric illness can obviously co-exist without either being a cause of the other [38]. Mortality from asthma is increased by depression, alcohol abuse, unemployment, schizophrenia and bereavement or family disruption [39].

Occupational asthma: exposure to a wide range of chemicals, plants or animal triggers in the workplace induce asthma in susceptible individuals. Subsequent exposure to even tiny amounts will usually result in further attacks. Such patients should usually be referred to a chest physician because of the serious implications for the asthmatic's future employment [40]. Typically symptoms will only occur at work. A written diagnosis should, with the asthmatic's consent, be sent to the employer who is obliged to inform the Employment Medical Advisory Services (EMAS) for workers in specific jobs or exposed to specific allergens. A list of these is available from EMAS. If the asthmatic declines to consent to the passing over of such information, the doctor can inform a medical officer of the EMAS or of an occupational health service if appropriate, in confidence.

Role of antibiotics: antibiotics are often given in acute exacerbations of asthma. They have a very limited role but many help clear an associated sinusitis. Acute exacerbations of asthma may result in the production of green or yellow sputum but this does not necessarily imply infection. Treatment with antibiotics of associated infections such as sinusitis must not be seen as a treatment for asthma, and antibiotics should never be given in preference to specific asthma therapy in acute exacerbations.

Acute severe asthma: guidelines for management [6,27]

Managing acute exacerbations which are very severe, even if adequate increases in medication have been taken, requires prompt treatment. Features of severe asthma include difficulty completing a sentence in a single breath, a respiratory rate of over 25/minute and a heart rate of over 110/minute, and a peak flow of less than 50% of best ever or predicted. Life-threatening features are a peak flow of less than 33% of best ever or predicted, cyanosis, a silent chest, bradycardia, hypotension, confusion, exhaustion or coma. In children, features of severe asthma are: a child too breathless to talk or feed, with a respiratory rate of over 50, a heart rate of over 140 and a peak flow of less than 50% best ever. Life-threatening features are a peak flow of less than 33% best ever, silent chest, cyanosis, fatigue, exhaustion, agitation and altered levels of consciousness. In infants there may be associated dehydration and vomiting. Treatment should be maximal and prompt.

Assessment	History, examination, peak flow if at all possible.
Oxygen	High flow and high concentration continuously until improvement has occurred and been maintained. Carbon dioxide retention is not aggravated by oxygen therapy in asthma.

Inhaled beta-agonists   Preferably given by nebulization, driven by oxygen if possible. Use salbutamol 2.5–5 mg or terbutaline 5–10 mg (children 2–5 mg); ipratropium 250–500 μg (children 100–500 μg) can be used concurrently with either.

Systemic steroids   Oral prednisolone 30–60 mg in one dose (children 2 mg/kg) or i.v. hydrocortisone 100–200 mg (children 4 mg/kg) if vomiting or unable to take orally.

Nebulized ipratropium bromide   Is best reserved for those asthmatics whose attacks are very severe when first seen, or who deteriorate or fail to improve rapidly when treated with the standard regimen of oxygen, steroids and beta-agonists.

Aminophylline   Intravenous aminophylline is of little additional benefit to asthmatics receiving maximum beta-agonists doses by nebulizer. Its use is best reserved for the indications listed above for ipratropium.

If improving   If clinical improvement follows and the peak flow increases to a minimum of 50% predicted and has improved by at least 20% from pre-treatment levels, advise 4-hourly high-dose inhaled beta-agonists, continue high-dose oral steroids taken as one dose each morning, and continue maintenance therapy at the dose indicated by the peak flow management plan or at double the usual dose. Review after 4 hours or so. Ensure that the asthmatic has a peak flow meter which they can use correctly and ensure they use it to monitor their progress every 4 hours or so. Ensure that they have clear, written instructions on how to recognize further deterioration and how and when to get further medical help, if necessary by dialling 999. If improvement is maintained, arrange further follow-up and review. Stop oral steroids once the peak flow has remained stable and at best-ever or predicted levels for at least 2 days.

If not improving   If clinical improvement is inadequate, or the peak flow is still less than 50% predicted or has not improved by at least 20% arrange immediate hospital admission. Whilst waiting for the ambulance, repeat the nebulized beta-agonist. If further deterioration occurs give subcutaneous bronchodilators: salbutamol 250–500 μg (children 5 μg/kg) or terbutaline 250–500 μg (children 10 μg/kg) or 1:1000 adrenaline 0.5 ml.

 If further deterioration occurs give intravenous bronchodilators: aminophylline 250 mg over 30 minutes (if not already on theophyllines) (children 5 μg/kg) or salbutamol 4 μg/kg over 10 minutes (not recommended for children) or terbutaline $250\,\mu$g over 10 minutes (children over the age of 2, $10\,\mu$g/kg). Do not give sedatives, antibiotics (unless clinically indicated) or physiotherapy.

Admission is also advised, although not necessarily via an emergency ambulance, if the asthmatic and/or their carers cannot safely cope with assessing the severity of the attack or cannot cope with adjusting the treatment. Similarly hospital admission should be arranged if the asthmatic has no access to a telephone or they are remote from sources of help. A lower threshold for admission is appropriate in patients seen in the latter part of the day, with recently worsening symptoms or recent onset of night symptoms, who have had previous severe attacks especially if they then rapidly deteriorated.

Follow-up

After every acute exacerbation follow-up should always be arranged. The trigger for the exacerbation should be identified if possible and advice given on possible future avoidance. The self-management plan should be reviewed or one instigated. Adjustment to the plan may be needed, especially the criteria for when and how to call for help. It may often be worth advising the use of oral steroids at an earlier stage of deterioration or even prophylactically if exposure to similar triggers is unavoidable in future. Obviously such patients should be prescribed a supply of oral steroids with reinforcing written instructions on when to start them, the dose, and when to stop them. In children use soluble prednisolone.

In small children or adults unable to use a peak flow meter, assessment will have to be solely on clinical grounds so more frequent reviews, especially initially, need to be made.

Success and failure

Success in asthma management occurs when all the aims of treatment are fulfilled for all asthmatics all the time. In practice if asthmatics' lives have been happier and of better quality, and any failure to fulfil their potential is not due to asthma or its treatment, then management is successful.

Failure is perhaps easier to assess. The following are indicators of failure.

Acute exacerbations: deaths, admissions to hospital, emergency nebulization, out of hours or other home visits are all indicators of failed management. If there was no self management plan to implement, then one must be agreed. If it was not adhered to, establish whether this was because the asthmatic did not understand how or when to use the peak flow meter, management plan, or inhalers, or when and how to alter treatment and call for help. If the asthmatic did call for help, were the treatment and advice given appropriate and the follow-up sufficient, including instructions on what to do after that contact? Although some asthmatics have severe, intractable asthma most failures of management are due to ignorance or poor communication by both asthmatics and their professional carers.

Common failings of management:
underdiagnosis of the disease;
underestimating the severity of symptoms and not determining the
    full extent to which an asthmatic is restricted by their disease;
underestimating the potential for improvement;
under use of preventative treatment, over-use of relievers: again, a
    communication and education problem;
poor inhaler technique;
lack of information for patients;
under-recognition of the asthmatics' emotional responses and needs;
non-compliance with agreed management plans;
and, perhaps the largest problem, the inconsistent quality of the care
    provided by different practices, GPs and nurses.

Summary

Asthma is a common disease that affects people of all ages. The symptoms and effects on people are very variable, but it is a common cause of physical, social and emotional morbidity as well as mortality.

Successful management is desirable and attainable. Asthma management is above all a problem for general practice. Successful management means forming a partnership between professional carers and asthmatics so that common aims of management can be agreed, as well as the means to implement those aims. Correct use of the many excellent drugs and delivery systems, especially combined with flexibility of treatment regimens, make this management more complex but more sophisticated. Successful asthma management is challenging and not always easy, but it is ultimately rewarding for asthmatics and their professional carers.

CHAPTER 3: THE ASTHMA CLINIC

The aims of the asthma clinic

The aims of the asthma clinic are:

1 To give patients the benefits of recent advances in the understanding of asthma.

2 To give patients the benefits of the excellent drug treatments which are available.

3 To deliver care by health professionals who have an interest and expertise in the management of asthma.

4 To improve the management of asthma so that deaths, inappropriate hospital admissions, absence from school or work and nebulizer use are all reduced.

5 To help asthmatics to understand the disease and its treatment and to reduce the adverse effects of asthma symptoms on their lives.

Thinking about an asthma clinic?

The prospect of setting up an asthma clinic may seem daunting. Doctors and nurses involved may feel that they lack the necessary clinical or organizational expertise required.

Practice nurses in particular may feel that they lack appropriate experience. They should not take on a role for which they do not feel themselves to be adequately prepared. But during the preparatory period for an asthma clinic many practice nurses begin involvement in asthma management at a modest level, for example by taking referrals from the general practitioner to check inhaler technique.

Such consultations provide an ideal opportunity for nurses to learn from patients about the effect of asthma on their lives and the lives of their carers. They also provide an opportunity to learn at first-hand about the advantages and disadvantages to patients of asthma medication and about the inhaler devices that are in most common use.

This valuable experience needs to be supported by training. A comprehensive list of training options is included later, but by exploiting some of the many sources of help available, the experience gained by contact with patients will soon be supported by an increase in knowledge and skills.

As the nurse gains confidence they will feel able to identify

49

suspected asthmatics among the rest of the practice population. On these occasions the nurse could initiate a period of peak flow monitoring, the result of which may be helpful to the doctor when making a diagnosis.

In this way involvement can begin at whatever level with which the nurse feels comfortable. It is not necessary to launch a full-scale asthma clinic from day one! Even this level of minimal involvement will benefit some patients and contribute to the establishment of a good relationship between nurse and patient. Indeed, taking on too much, too soon would be inviting problems and would jeopardize the success of the long-term aims of improving asthma management in the practice.

Certain pharmaceutical companies are excellent sources of educational material for professionals, asthmatics and their carers. Their involvement at this stage will ensure a supply of demonstration inhaler devices and other equipment.

What is involved

The people

General practitioners must provide the time, enthusiasm, investment of practice resources and of money, and the education of themselves and the primary health team.

Practice nurses must be educated and provide enthusiasm, skill and knowledge. In most clinics it is the practice nurse who sees most asthmatics most of the time. She is the key worker and must be supported and respected as such.

The practice manager and receptionist must be actively involved from the creation of the data base, to setting up call/recall systems, organizing clinic logistics and ensuring the smooth running of the clinic.

The things

The clinic will need a room, printed forms, a supply of demonstration devices, a supply of peak flow meters, and supplies of educational and resource materials. It is important to have peak flow charts to give to asthmatics to record their home peak flows. An accurate height measure and charts or wheels to estimate predicted peak flows are also necessary.

The principles of setting up a clinic

Involving colleagues

Involve the whole practice in the project. Share ideas and pay the most attention to the more reluctant members of the team, raising their interest by increasing their confidence and knowledge and by being realistic in the possible rewards and demands — financial, organizational and time. Enthuse about the potential benefits of a clinic for asthmatics and the practice.

Doctors and nurses may sometimes find that this enthusiasm to improve the management of asthma in their practice by establishing a clinic is not shared by their colleagues. Nurses may have to work particularly hard if they are to demonstrate to their medical colleagues the value of better informed and structured care for asthmatic patients. Neither should nurses be afraid to demonstrate their interest and involvement in asthma care by noting any intervention in the medical records. Enquiring about symptoms, checking inhaler techniques or peak flow readings and recording them in the notes may stimulate reluctant colleagues to take a greater interest in asthma management.

Diagnostic criteria

Agree diagnostic criteria and apply them, using internationally accepted criteria for diagnosis [1, 2] and accept that asthma is primarily a chronic inflammatory disease.

Find out who they are

Identify all asthmatics in the practice and keep a register. If the practice keeps summary cards or morbidity indexes the task is easier, especially if the practice is computerized. Other, slower methods include random or systematic note scrutiny, looking for key words, such as *wheeze, still coughing, coughs at night, salbutamol* etc. Scrutiny of all repeat prescription requests will identify most of a practice's asthmatics fairly rapidly as the drugs used in asthma are rarely of use in other conditions, except chronic bronchitis. Judicious control of repeat prescriptions is also an easy way of increasing attendances at clinics.

Future identification

Label each asthmatic's notes so that future identification is easy. This can be as a separate register, or by marking the age-sex register or the notes. Buy or design an asthma summary card so baseline data on each asthmatic can be accumulated (an example is shown in Fig. 3.1). If the system allows, design a practice defined asthma summary and follow-up screen on the computer.

Asthma clinic protocol

Establish a clinic protocol. It is best if there is a sense of ownership by all those who will be involved in the care of asthmatics, so all should have a say in its design. Involve the practice nurses, community nurses, school nurses, health visitors and pharmacists at an early stage. Agree criteria for chronic long-term management, acute management, intra-practice referrals, drug treatments and follow-up intervals. Do not be afraid of altering the protocols by agreement

CURRENT TREATMENT

Date								

ANNUAL REVIEW

Date						

Asthma Summary Card

Name	
D. of B.	Occupation 1.
Age at 1st Diagnosis	2.
Family History: asthma	3.
hayfever	4.
eczema	5.
Allergies: aspirin	other drugs
other	
Smoker: self	
(No./day) others in home	
TRIGGERS URTI	other infections
exercise	dust
others	
Type of Asthma	
Hospital Admissions 1.	3. 5. 7.
(dates) 2.	4. 6. 8.
Oral Steroids 1.	2. 3. 4.
(dates) 5.	6. 7. 8.
9.	10. 11. 12.
13.	14. 15. 16.
Expected PEFR: date	
EPEFR	
PEFR meter date	
owned:	
Self Management Plan Given (date)	
Explanations Given: (date)	
Literature Given: (dates)	
Additional Information:	

Fig. 3.1 An example of a practice-designed asthma summary card.

in the light of experience. Be prepared for increased prescribing costs — involvement at an early stage of the local pharmacists and hospitals as well as the medical and pharmaceutical advisors of the Family Health Service Authority or Health Board is strongly recommended.

Review

Review all of the above regularly. Do not expect instant perfection but be prepared to be flexible and to alter one's plans in the light of experience.

Education

Educate, educate, educate: the doctors about opportunistic diagnosis, screening and referral to the clinic, but also on sharing the management with other colleagues in primary care and with the asthmatics themselves.

The nurses and doctors about asthma and its management. The Asthma Training Centre in Stratford and the Asthma Management Centre in Liverpool provide excellent distance-learning and in-house training. Many FHSAs and Health Boards run local courses and employ facilitators especially for the community care of asthma. Many local postgraduate centres will also run courses or talks. Certain pharmaceutical companies also provide help in the form of training, educating, long-term back-up and encouragement.

Protected time

It needs to be recognized that if a clinic is to be successful in achieving its stated aims, protected time will need to be set aside. As well as time

Table 3.1 Checklists for the clinic

ASTHMA CLINIC PROTOCOLS
Topics to include:
Aims of the clinic
Identification and registration of patients
Record keeping
Priority patients
Responsibility of the practice nurse and general practitioner
Referral criteria: inside and outside practice
Recall procedure
Audit

ASTHMA CLINIC TASKS
Compile and update the asthma register
Patient education, especially initially
Teach and check inhaler and peak flow techniques
Take a formal history
Be able to identify poorly controlled asthmatics by taking a careful history
Teach and supervise home peak flow monitoring
Provide general information and counselling
Establish follow-up procedures
Establish an intra-practice referral system, and one for external referrals

---

for the clinic, time will be required for record-keeping, call and re-call, review and audit.

If nurses are to take on the running of an asthma clinic, it follows that they will need more hours if their work is to be extended.

Recent changes within general practice have resulted in payments to general practitioners who are able to show that good quality care is being provided for their asthmatic patients. The principles discussed in this section, if applied, will allow such payments. However, care may be provided at individual consultations although many practices will find it more satisfactory to see most patients in a dedicated clinic setting.

Talking to asthmatics

Establishing a relationship

Obviously asthmatics will vary in their ability to understand and absorb the information given to them. The doctor or nurse should be aware of the need to adjust the amount and level of information given to the patient.

Newly diagnosed asthmatics or parents of asthmatic children may be initially resistant to accepting a diagnosis of asthma. It may be reassuring to explain to them that advances in the understanding of asthma by the medical world, and awareness of how common it is, has lead to better diagnosis and more appropriate use of the medication available. Both patients and parents of asthmatic children may be aware of asthmatics in the past who have had severe asthma and may find this a frightening prospect for themselves or their children.

The media play a role in the public perception of asthma. Whilst some positive messages about the treatment of asthma are conveyed, asthma is often dramatically portrayed as a severe frightening and life-threatening condition. It can sometimes be all of these things. But this impression needs to be counteracted with positive messages that most asthma is mild and that most symptoms are preventable.

Doctors and nurses will be aware of the prevalence of negative feelings held by the general public about the use of steroids. Patients may be aware of people who have been treated with long-term oral steroids in the past and who may have suffered severe adverse effects. All these anxieties may need to be addressed in the weeks after diagnosis and indeed where asthma is only suspected. Reassurance and support at this stage is crucial to forming a good relationship with the patient. It is important to foster an atmosphere in which the doctor and nurse will be able to provide continuing education and treatment which will be accepted by the patient.

An asthma clinic will allow doctors and nurses to build up a good relationship with their patients. Compliance with treatment is essential for effective symptom control and compliance is significantly improved when care is delivered by doctors and nurses with whom the patient has a good one-to-one relationship.

Encouraging a positive attitude

Be prepared to listen to the asthmatic talk about their symptoms and of the effects of asthma on their life. Pay attention to problems of low self-esteem and of prejudice, perceived or real. Compliance with therapy will never be possible if imposed from above, it is better to agree management. Agreement can be reached by mutual understanding and by education. Be especially careful to enquire into specific symptoms and factors of wellbeing.

Inform patients that asthma is common, incurable but eminently treatable. Patients should expect to lead fully active lives and if this is not the case, they should return for advice. The disease need not be a disability or a stigma. Tell the patient that ultimately they can be in control of their disease and its treatment, and that poorly treated and managed asthma may be a dangerous disease but if the asthmatic and the professional carers form an understanding partnership it should not become dangerous but be more of a minor nuisance. Parents of asthmatic children should be told to expect normal growth and development of their child; not all children by any means *grow out of it*, but some do appear to.

What is asthma?

Inform the patient about asthma, how common it is, that it can start at any age, and that family history may be relevant but is not a prerequisite for the disease. Tell the patient that asthma is a disease where the lining of the lung is abnormally sensitive so it readily becomes inflamed. This causes it to swell, producing thicker, stickier phlegm and irritability of the muscles in the small tubes of the lungs causing them to be twitchy and go into spasm. As a result of the inflammation and muscle spasm the tubes are narrowed causing the symptoms of cough, chest tightness, breathlessness and wheeze. Sometimes either the inflammation or the muscle spasm predominates but usually both are important.

Trigger factors

Asthmatics are often aware of what triggers their asthma, but discussion may uncover previously unsuspected triggers. It is helpful to explain how the triggers produce the symptoms described above and to discuss how these might be avoided. Knowledge about the role of the house-dust mite as a trigger is particularly important. Soft furnishings, bedding and books in children's bedrooms may be contributing to night symptoms and practical advice in this area may be helpful. Obviously asthmatics should be vigorously discouraged from smoking and children should not be passively exposed to cigarette smoke.

Sharing the aims of management

Inform asthmatics about the aims of management. The concept of a clinic in general practice may be new to them, particularly if run by a nurse. A simple explanation of the general aims of the management of asthma will help asthmatics to know what to expect from their treatment.

Understanding the medication

Asthmatics should expect to lead a normal or near normal life-style, untroubled by their asthma symptoms or their treatment. Inform the patient of the difference between reliever, preventer and protector drugs, when to take them, how to take them and when to increase and decrease them. It is often some time before patients fully absorb the concept of the different types of asthma medication. It may be necessary to repeat this information in different ways at different consultations.

Inhaler devices: selecting the most appropriate inhaler device is vital as it will help to ensure good drug delivery to the lungs. Patient involvement with choice of inhaler device may help compliance but the nurse is in a position to make an informed recommendation. It is essential to review their use of the device regularly because technique may deteriorate.

Peak flow meters

Show the patient how to use a peak flow meter, explaining what it measures, what level to expect, what various sub-optimal levels mean, and what to do at various lower levels and when to call for help.

Adjusting treatment

From the early days of diagnosis, patients need to know how to adjust their treatment. At times of increased risk, such as with a cold or other infection, cold weather or prolonged exercise, those on relievers only, should increase the doses to the maximum or start regular preventative treatment; those on preventative treatment should double the doses and perhaps take a reliever regularly [1].

Whatever the increase it should be maintained for at least 48 hours after the risk has passed.

Recognizing
deterioration

Good asthma management requires that patients should know how to recognize a deterioration in lung function. Long-term sufferers often tolerate symptoms and accept them as part of their condition.

The patient must be aware of what may seem like trivial symptoms such as increased need for reliever treatment, poor response to reliever treatment, increase in night symptoms or daytime chest tightness, may require action to prevent a severe or even life-threatening attack.

When doctors and nurses are in regular contact with individuals, as in an asthma clinic, they can be sensitive to that person's willingness or competence to recognize deterioration and educate them accordingly. Use of a peak flow meter by suitably educated patients results in better recognition of the significance of symptoms [3].

Specific things to say about drugs

Short-acting beta-
agonist inhalers

These work by relaxing the muscles in the bronchi and opening up the airways. This relieves the asthma symptoms, so they are known as *relievers*. Use the inhaler as prescribed and alter its dose and frequency as advised.

*Side-effects of inhaled
beta-agonists*

These are rare but can include headaches, palpitations, tremor, nausea, cramp and hypokalaemia.

Inhaled steroids

Steroid inhalers work by reducing inflammation in the lungs. The inflammation results in sticky, thick phlegm, swollen linings of the bronchi and ultimately irritability and spasm of the bronchial muscles. Preventing the inflammation prevents the chain of events and therefore the symptoms, so they are known as *preventers*. They may possibly protect the lungs from long-term damage. Steroid inhalers are designed for long-term use and are usually very effective and relatively safe. They are designed to keep you well so take them regularly even if you have been very well for some time. The amount of steroid absorbed if you are using the inhaler correctly is very small and in no way comparable to the amounts taken as tablets. In children, low to medium doses have not been shown to inhibit growth. In higher doses there is less certainty, but severe asthma certainly does affect growth, so the treatment is better than the disease. Take regularly, using the inhaler as advised, and adjust the dose when appropriate according to the instructions given.

*Side-effects of inhaled
steroids*

Oral thrush and vocal dysfunction may be a problem. Risks are reduced if the mouth is rinsed after inhalation. Good advice is to inhale the drugs before cleaning the teeth — this aids compliance and ensures oropharyngeal deposits are washed away. Both side-effects are reversible.

Oral steroids

Steroid tablets are stronger and longer acting than inhaled steroid preparations, as the dose is much larger. They are the most effective anti-inflammatory drugs we have and so are the most powerful way to stop a severe or potentially severe asthma attack. Always take the complete daily dose in one go, and continue the tablets until the course is finished, unless the doctor or nurse has advised otherwise.

Side-effects of oral steroids

The side-effects of short-term oral steroids (less than one course per month) include increased appetite and hence weight-gain, bad dreams and mood changes, usually euphoria. Certain people, especially the elderly, may experience frank psychiatric symptoms especially pseudo-dementia and personality change. These effects are reversible on stopping the drug.

Side-effects of long-term oral steroids are multiple and include thinning of the skin, osteoporosis, diabetes, redistribution of body fat, muscle wasting, and Addisonian type effects. Steroids used in asthma are not the same as the anabolic steroids abused by some athletes.

Theophyllines and oral beta-agonist

These relax bronchial smooth muscle. Sustained-release formulations will provide long-term protection if taken regularly. Patients should take them regularly even if they feel well.

Side-effects of theophyllines

Theophyllines commonly cause sleep disturbance. Some people, especially children, become hyperactive. Gastro-intestinal symptoms can occur, as can palpitations and tremor. Up to one-third of children on theophyllines suffer some side-effects [1].

Side-effects of oral beta-agonists

These include headaches, tremor, palpitations, nausea, cramps and hypokalaemia.

Cromoglycate and nedocromil

These are anti-inflammatory inhaled drugs which modify the allergic reaction responsible for the resulting inflammation and bronchial muscle spasm in some asthmatics. They are preventers, and patients should know that they must be taken regularly, even when the patient is well.

Side-effects of cromoglycate and nedocromil

There are next to no side-effects from these drugs. Coughing on inhaling cromoglycate can be a nuisance. Some patients cannot tolerate the taste of nedocromil.

Salmeterol	Salmeterol is a long-acting beta-agonist bronchodilator which will help protect the lungs from the effects of triggers. It is especially useful for night-time symptoms and prevention of activity-induced asthma. Patients should take it regularly twice daily even when well. Other preventer treatment should not be stopped. Salmeterol is a protector.
Side-effects of salmeterol	Side-effects are rare and are those of other inhaled beta-agonists.
General points about drugs	There are a few general points about asthma drugs that should form the specific information which patients are given. 1 Addiction does not occur with asthma drugs. However, some asthmatics may never be able to stop their treatment as the asthma would get worse. This is because of the asthma, not its treatment. 2 Tolerance to the drugs used in asthma rarely ever occurs. 3 Side-effects may occur with all drugs but are not usually a particular problem for asthmatics. Side-effects should be discussed, including ways to diminish them, before prescribing. It is important to emphasize that there are millions of people taking asthma drugs for many years, and most have no problems from side-effects. Patients need to know that side-effects could occur and if they become a great problem, the patient will need to inform the prescriber so that alternative therapy can be prescribed.

The clinic

Once an asthmatic has been identified they are invited to the clinic and the fact of the invitation recorded. Allow 20 to 40 minutes for the first appointment and on no account attempt to cover all the aspects of asthma and its management.

At this initial appointment:
register the patient;
measure height and weight;
explain the purpose of the clinic (it is not just for ill asthmatics!);
complete the summary or database card including past history,
    family history, current and past medications for asthma;
teach and check inhaler technique;
teach and check peak flow meter reading;
assess severity of asthma from recent history, drug use and lifestyle;
identify triggers;
arrange a subsequent appointment in a week or two.

At subsequent appointments:
explore the patient's assessment of their disease;
explain about the disease and its management;
ask about symptom control. Be as specific as possible. Ask especially about days off work or school, night symptoms, exercise tolerance, limitations — however 'minor' — of daily living;
review the current management especially the types of drugs used, the patient's understanding of these drugs, inhaler technique, doses and how well the patient is able to comply with the regimen;
review the trigger factors and, if feasible, their avoidance;
check peak flow readings; explain the concept of peak flow readings; prescribe a meter if appropriate;
make sure the patient knows how to recognize deterioration, how to respond and when to call for help;
educate, listen to the patient and explain where necessary;
arrange a follow-up.

If appropriate, now or later, assess:
the need for a peak flow led self management plan;
the need for a symptom card.

Subsequent appointments should cover symptom control, inhaler technique, knowledge and confidence as to when to increase treatment, how to do it and when to call for help. Listen to the asthmatic, answer any questions, enquire about how asthma and its management may be affecting the life-style of the asthmatic. Use every consultation to listen, to educate, to explain. Once stable and secure, a short checklist of key information can be used. This could even be made into a rubber stamp for recording in the patients notes.

Asthma
Subjective . . . .
Night symptoms . . . .
Day symptoms . . . .
Exercise limitations . . . .
Acute attacks . . . .
Days off school/work . . . .
Bronchodilator use . . . .
Peak flow/best ever PF . . . .
Knows when and how:
   to step up treatment . . . .
   to step down treatment . . . .
   to call for help . . . .

Technique:
    Pf . . . .
    Inhaler . . . .
Follow-up . . . .

Special considerations

Peak flow charts: All asthmatics capable of using the meter should know their expected or best ever peak flow. Most asthmatics should own a peak flow meter. It is desirable that asthmatics monitor their peak flows at home, especially in the following circumstances:
newly diagnosed asthmatic;
recent step-up or step-down in chronic management;
recent exacerbation;
recent change of medication or inhaler device;
recent change of job, house or possible trigger (e.g. pet acquired).

An example which combines peak flow readings with a symptom diary is shown in Figure 3.2.

Self-management plans: it is not much use monitoring a peak flow without knowing how to react to changes. A peak flow led self-management plan allows the asthmatic to alter their treatment in relation to the severity of the asthma as measured by peak flow readings. This allows the asthmatic more control of the disease and management, increasing compliance and the beneficial effects of management. Examples are shown in Figures 2.2 and 2.3.

The annual review: every asthmatic should be called for review at least annually. At the review every asthmatic should be asked about symptoms, and bronchodilator reliever use, and have their peak flow measured. The inhaler and peak flow techniques should be checked and altered if necessary. In each case it should be ascertained that the asthmatic knows how and when to alter treatment and when to call for help.

Subsequent follow-up should be agreed between the asthmatic and nurse or doctor. The interval between follow-ups will vary with each asthmatic, and with how stable and well they have been. It is important to ensure that the clinic includes a mixture of follow-up appointments and new patient initial assessments. It is all too easy to end up recalling the same patients back to the clinic. The notes of all asthmatics should be reviewed annually. Those who have not

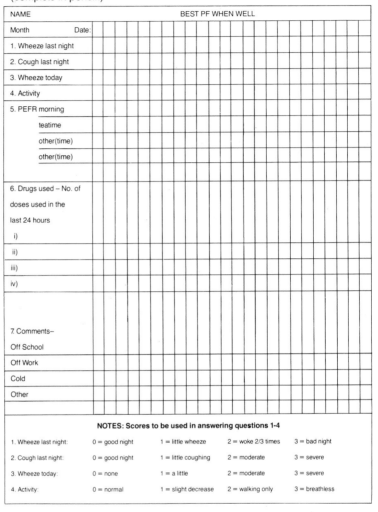

Symptom Card for Asthma

(complete in pencil!)

NAME											BEST PF WHEN WELL															
Month Date:																										
1. Wheeze last night																										
2. Cough last night																										
3. Wheeze today																										
4. Activity																										
5. PEFR morning																										
teatime																										
other(time)																										
other(time)																										
6. Drugs used – No. of doses used in the last 24 hours																										
i)																										
ii)																										
iii)																										
iv)																										
7. Comments– Off School																										
Off Work																										
Cold																										
Other																										

NOTES: Scores to be used in answering questions 1-4

1. Wheeze last night:	0 = good night	1 = little wheeze	2 = woke 2/3 times	3 = bad night
2. Cough last night:	0 = good night	1 = little coughing	2 = moderate	3 = severe
3. Wheeze today:	0 = none	1 = a little	2 = moderate	3 = severe
4. Activity:	0 = normal	1 = slight decrease	2 = walking only	3 = breathless

Fig. 3.2 A chart combining peak flow readings with a symptom diary.

attended should be called for an annual review. A summary of how to set up the clinic is shown in Figure 3.3.

Some asthmatics may have required no treatment for some time. Should they be reviewed or should they be deleted from the register? There are no rules! A useful concept is to categorize some asthmatics into a 'Quiescent asthma' category. These asthmatics are not deleted from the register but are not called for review. This ensures that no-one slips through the net of being called an ex-asthmatic and receiving what may be inappropriate management for possible asthma. Similarly it is not wasting everyone's time by reviewing

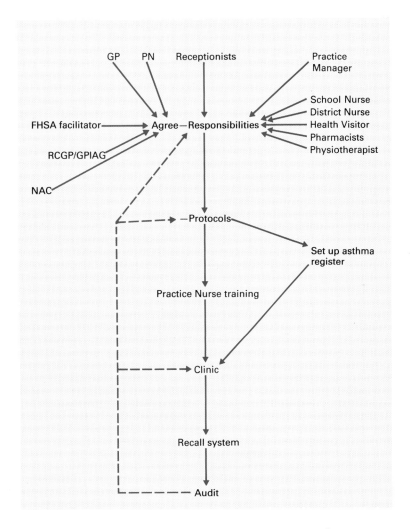

Fig. 3.3 How to set up an asthma clinic.

completely well, untreated people. Criteria for entry to this category are:

previously diagnosed asthmatic;

no treatment with any anti-asthma drugs for two years or more;

no attendance in the last year with any chest symptoms, allowing for two episodes of self limiting day-time cough;

the last three peak flow readings have all been at least 80% predicted.

Advantages and disadvantages of a clinic

Advantages for the patient:
time to talk and learn;
increased self confidence and self-esteem;

decreased reliance on professionals;
increased good health;
increased compliance with treatment.

For the primary health care team:
increased professional satisfaction;
decreased out of hours work;
reduced prescribing costs for non-asthma treatments for respiratory
    complaints, and for some antibiotics.

Disadvantages:
work may increase initially leading to:
disruption to the practice;
less time, less space, less money;
'higher' prescribing costs for asthma treatments.

Why bother . . .
1 With the register — need to plan resources, and effective care
audit; need to identify asthmatics and implement a call/recall system.
2 With individual assessment — easy access to information, identify
those most at risk of having severe acute asthma, increased compliance with treatment and follow-up.
3 With regular review — decreased morbidity and mortality,
increased patient and professional satisfaction. Decreased time off
work and hospitalization for the patient, less out-of-hours work for
the doctor.
4 With self-management — increased patient control; decreased
work, out-of-hours visits for the doctor. Increased satisfaction all
round.
   Specific advantages to specific people are shown in Table 3.2

Referrals

Why should there be referrals by the primary health care team to
other agencies? To whom? In what circumstances?
   When considering referral of asthmatics' there are three factors:
the referrer;
the asthmatic;
the person to whom the asthmatic is referred.

The referrer: initially the inexperienced general practitioner will feel
more secure referring seemingly difficult cases for a second opinion
on management. As their confidence and expertise grows, the

Table 3.2 Specific advantages of an asthma clinic for different people

Person	Present involvement	Involvement with clinic	Future benefit	How can he/she wreck it
GP	Manage haphazardly	Manage logically and carefully	Increased care; decreased work	Ignore protocols; unsupportive
Patient	Reactive care	Proactive care	Decreased illness	Fail to keep appointments
Nurse	Nil	In charge of clinic	Increased care; increased involvement (increased work)	Ignore protocols; lack of confidence; lack of competence; lack of training
Practice Manager	Nil	Organize clinics	Involvement	Poor admin.
Reception	Nil	Ensure smooth running of clinic	Decreased 'extras' emergencies	Inability to adapt
School/ work	Nil	Support and encouragement; recruitment	Less absenteeism less disruption	Not allowing treatment at work or school; not allowing patient to live normally
Hospital	Reactive	Supportive	Fewer admissions; fewer out-patients	Withdrawal of support; not allowing sharing of care
Pharmacist	Reactive	Supportive	Well clients	Excessive commercial focus
		Monitoring	Enhance professional role	Disinterest
		Back-up	Job satisfaction	

referral rates will usually fall. Eventually the level of expertise of the general practitioner may almost match that of the expert, and in some aspects exceed it.

The asthmatic: when is it advisable to refer to hospital out-patients?

1 Adults: diagnostic doubt — self explanatory. Occupational asthma — the diagnosis may have profound effects. With other illnesses — combinations such as severe rheumatoid arthritis (with a 'fixed' chest wall), or severe ischaemic heart disease or heart failure may make a specialist's input desirable. Severe asthma requiring step 5 treatment – to confirm that everything has been done to help the asthmatic.

2 Children: diagnostic doubt. Associated systemic disease, e.g. cystic fibrosis, congenital heart disease. Severe asthma, certainly if requiring step 4 or 5 treatment.

The person to whom the asthmatic is referred: not all district general hospitals have a chest physician (although most do); certainly many lack a paediatrician with an interest in asthma. If at all possible it makes sense to refer to an expert with an appropriate interest.

When should the nurse running the clinic refer back to the general practitioner?

when treatment is failing despite full compliance and good inhaler technique;

after an acute attack which was severe;

whenever a course of oral steroids has been started or if a first course is needed;

whenever the nurse is worried;

whenever there are persistent side-effects to drugs;

when symptoms appear unrelated to asthma;

whenever a patient asks to see a doctor.

When should asthmatics be referred to the clinic?

when an agreed management protocol has been accepted;

all asthmatics should eventually be referred, preferably when well or stable.

There should normally be a doctor available to the clinic at all times.

The patients' views

Ideally clinics should take place outside normal surgery appointments, so as to avoid undue contact with other patients' respiratory infections in the waiting room.

The nurse should be trained in asthma care and fully up to date with all available medication and methods of administration. I would expect to be treated as a mature adult and not as a 6-year-old (as has been my experience).

As a patient it has been necessary for me to attend hospital clinics regularly, and I have always felt that the doctor I see not only cares for my asthma condition, but cares about me also, and naturally I would hope for the same sort of care at my GP's surgery.

I was diagnosed as having asthma in my 60th year and had I experienced the same care then, that I have received in the past few years I feel I would have coped better initially. When a change of medication is advised, a further appointment should be made to check on progress. [Mrs B Oakley, Chairperson, Swindon Branch, National Asthma Campaign]

As a mother of two boys aged 11 years and 9 years who both have asthma, I would like to be able to go to an asthma clinic to have their condition and health monitored at regular intervals. I would like to see a nurse who has been trained in the care of asthma and knows exactly what the asthma treatment is and which treatment should be taken and how. She should keep up to date with the new inhalers and medications available to patients. She should be able to show the patient and carer how inhalers should be taken properly. At each clinic the patient should be monitored by peak flow readings and given advice on their medication. Perhaps if everything was OK the nurse would be able to write repeat prescriptions [unfortunately this is not possible]. [Mrs C Gallagher, Secretary, Swindon Branch, National Asthma Campaign]

The things I would like to see at an asthma clinic include separate waiting areas for patients (to avoid cross infection); sensible timings of appointments (to avoid delays and long waiting times); and follow-up appointments made by the nurse (to avoid queuing at reception again to make a further appointment).

I also think it would be a good idea for the nurse to give the patient aims for the future, e.g. if a child is very young and on a nebulizer, to show the parent what type of inhaler to which the child will progress. In my experience, I was always the one to suggest progression to a new inhaler.

More information could also be given regarding the possible side-effects of the different drugs used. For instance, my daughter actually started sleeping through the night at 5 years of age and this coincided with her being taken off a slow-release theophylline preparation. I also found her general behaviour was an awful lot better.

It would also be a good idea for the nurse to advise the patient of the National Asthma Campaign; its Helpline and details of branch meetings. I would like to see all asthma clinic nurses trained on up to date methods of controlling asthma and perhaps visiting the schools/teachers of asthmatic children who attend their clinics to offer advice regarding their care at school. [Mrs Wendy Watts, member Swindon Branch, National Asthma Campaign]

The role of the pharmacist

Be involved with the local practices; try to encourage the setting up of asthma clinics, and to be involved in drawing up protocols. The pharmacist can play a very valuable role in identifying poorly controlled patients and referring them to the clinic, in teaching and checking patients' inhaler technique and in educating and counselling patients about their asthma and treatment.

Be aware of how common and variable asthma is; of the importance of preventative treatment, of the symptoms of asthma; of the practicalities of peak flow monitoring; of how inhalers work and how to check asthmatics' techniques, and when to do so; that cough mixtures have no part to play in asthma management; that certain over-the-counter medicines may interact with asthma treatment, especially those containing theophyllines.

Be alert to the symptoms in the undiagnosed, the under-treated and the unaware.

Be supportive of asthmatics, helping to educate and monitor them and by distributing literature and leaflets; of the local clinics by promoting attendance; of good asthma management by discouraging inappropriate use of proprietary medicines, and by not promoting antibiotics as an asthma treatment. The net result will be increased professional satisfaction, appropriate dispensing and sales, and a happier, healthier, more loyal clientele.

Summary

There are good treatments for asthma, and its management has now become more sophisticated. However, the organization of delivery of care is as important as the quality of care given. Asthma clinics if properly organized and run, can greatly improve the care of asthma to the benefit of asthmatics and their carers and also of health care professionals.

CHAPTER 4: AUDIT

Introduction

Audit is nothing more than looking at what one is doing and comparing it with what one would like to be doing and trying to make the two identical.

Asthma is well suited to general practice audit as it is common, and there are recognized, measurable outcomes and processes. Asthma audit should involve the team which is involved in asthma care, and not be the responsibility of only one member. However a team leader or co-ordinator is advisable although this position can rotate amongst the team. The cardinal rules of all audit are to keep it simple, to keep it specific and to keep it relevant. As practices' experience grows, audit can move from the very simple to the more complex.

There are three parts to a successful asthma audit [1].

1 Set objectives for asthma care, primarily for outcome, but also for process.

2 Measure how far the objectives have been met.

3 Redefine the objectives or alter the provision of care to achieve the objectives.

4 Re-audit.

Subjects to audit: some ideas

Some ideas of subjects to audit:

Measures of fact: e.g. practice prevalence of asthma: clinic attendances.

Measures of process: e.g. how many asthmatics own a peak flow meter? How many have had a peak flow measurement recorded in the last year? How many are on inhaled steroids or anti-inflammatories, or other measures of appropriate treatment?

Measures of outcome: e.g. how many nebulizations, home visits, or emergency admissions there were per month, daily/nocturnal symptom scores, inhaler technique ability, compliance with medication, time off work/school.

The audit process

Having decided which areas of asthma management to audit, the practice must set criteria and agree standards. These should be agreed by the asthma team and not imposed from above. Such standards for the examples mentioned above might be:

Measures of fact: to establish their practice prevalence for adults and children and compare with national rates; to see every asthmatic at least annually;

Measures of process: to achieve 50% of asthmatics owning a peak flow meter; to have recorded a peak flow reading in the last year for asthmatics aged 5 or more; to have 100% asthmatics who require more than four relieving inhalers a year also taking a preventative inhaler;

Measures of outcome: to achieve no hospital admissions due to acute asthma, no emergency nebulizations and no home visits, 100% of asthmatics with *good* inhaler technique and no asthmatics suffering nocturnal symptoms.

Outcome audit is particularly important for asthma as the aim of management and treatment should be to keep all patients symptom-free and able to lead a life unrestricted by symptoms.

The next stage is to collect and organize the data. Data retrieval depends on data input. At this stage it is often necessary to review the asthma protocol and insert or delete the need to record certain data. Adequate data recording is essential for all audit but it is often not until audit is undertaken that deficiencies of data input become apparent.

The data then need to be analysed. The results achieved need to be compared with the standards set. Discrepancies should be highlighted and attempts should be made to identify the causes of any non-achievement [2]. For example, if the practice has an adult prevalence of 14% and a childhood prevalence of 6% against national estimates of 5% and 10% respectively [3], why is this? Are the diagnostic standards inappropriately wide for adults and narrow for children? Similarly low ownership of peak flow meters may be due to lack of awareness on the part of the professional carers about how useful they can be. The subject may have been omitted from the clinic protocols. Failure to meet the outcome standards may be due to faulty clinical protocols, inadequate monitoring, training or education or inappropriate prescribing, poor use of self-management plans or inappropriate advice or any combination [4].

Having identified the causes of non-achievement of standards, changes should be implemented so that they can be achieved. Unrealistic standards may need to be modified. For example, the practice may feel that never using emergency nebulizations is unrealistic or may endanger some asthmatics by encouraging the withholding of appropriate treatment. It may be necessary to lower or raise standards. If the standard was appropriate but unmet, changes in the provision of care must be made. If the practice prevalence of asthma varies widely from national estimates, the diagnostic criteria should be reviewed to ensure they agree with other agreed standards. If attendance at the asthma clinic is low, is this because it is held at an inconvenient time or place? Is failure to review every asthmatic annually due to inadequate provision of clinic time or poor organization so that not all are called and recalled? If too few asthmatics are using preventative treatment is it because the treatment protocols are wrong, or is the training of those running the clinic inadequate, or is the advice not being complied with by asthmatics? If outcome measures fall short of the standards is this due to poor care, to good care which is badly organized, or do the practice's asthmatics have dreadful asthma despite excellent care and management?

The final stage is to implement changes to protocols, procedures, standards, organization of care or provision of care, and then to re-evaluate, monitor progress and re-audit. It is only by looking critically at the effects of change that we can evaluate that change. Not all change is necessarily good!

Audit should be a continuing process. Eventually in an ideal world all one's initial standards would be met, so they would have to be raised. The provision of asthma care should therefore continue to improve and improve.

Audit can be uplifting, interesting or sometimes dispiriting. It is better, especially initially, to keep audit very simple and to confine oneself to asking simple questions which involve easy data collection and analysis and which have fairly straight forward causes of non-achievement and where it is easy to make small, beneficial changes. At first it is also best to audit simple aspects of asthma care that one thinks one is doing well, to provide positive feedback for the whole team. As confidence increases so can the complexity of audits, and one can concentrate more on the aspects that are probably being done less well, and therefore more in need of change. A more experienced, confident team can cope with negative feedback.

Does audit show that asthma clinics make any difference to the provision of asthma care? The answer is probably that they do but whether the improvement comes from having nurse-run asthma clinics or from the practice developing an interest in asthma, with protocols, self-management plans and peak flow meter use, is difficult to know [5, 6]. It is more certain that patient education alone is insufficient to alter morbidity [7, 8]. An example of a complex audit has been included [9].

An example of an asthma audit, Elm Tree Surgery, Shrivenham 1991

Ultimate goal: to keep all our asthmatics well at all times.

Aims

To measure the process.

A To find the current prevalence of asthma in the practice, and to compare it with last year's and the national prevalence.

B To quantify the completion of the summary cards

C To quantify peak flow recordings made on each patient and to see whether the peak flow readings reflected good control.

D To see how easy it is to identify the current maintenance treatment.

E To assess the appropriateness of that treatment.

F To look closely at those patients not seen at all during 1990.

To measure the outcome.

G To quantify the number of hospital admissions for asthma.

H To quantify the number of oral steroid courses.

J   To see whether patients requiring nebulization or admission were managed optimally before that event.

Introduction

This is the second annual audit of asthma, and covers the 1990 calendar year. In the first (1989) we audited the practice prevalence, the recording of triggers and type of asthma, and the drugs used (measure of process). We also audited the peak flow recordings and hospital admissions (measures of outcome). We agreed to use the reverse of the summary card to record the current maintenance treatment, to update the card regularly and to record standard features at each clinic consultation.

Results
(A) Prevalence

1990

| Age | Male | Female | Total | % asthmatics in that age group | | % increase |
				1990	1989	1989–90
0–4	15	20	35	10.7	10.1	5.9
5–14	39	41	80	10.4	10.2	2.0
15–64	97	87	184	5.0	4.0	25.0
65+	18	28	46	6.7	4.2	32.6
Total	169	176	345	6.1	4.7	22.0

Discussion

It is obvious that the largest increase is in adult asthma, especially the elderly. This in part reflects the fact that initially we focused more on children with possible asthma symptoms but we have now identified and diagnosed most of the asthmatic children. As we have an annual turnover of 40% of children under five, we are either diagnosing patients new to the practice at a similar rate or the child's previous GP has done so.

We are now focusing more on the adults. The initial delay may have been due to focusing on children to the exclusion of adults, which we have now rectified. Some of the increase may have been due to a true rise in incidence but it is difficult to postulate that an increase would affect only adults.

National prevalence figures are unknown but the current popular figures are generally accepted as about 10% for children and 5% for adults. Our figures, then, show the prevalence of asthma for our patients to be in line with the national average. Thus we can argue that our diagnostic criteria are appropriate and our means of identifying asthmatics are working well.

(B) Assessment

Summary card: a crude measure of whether each patient has had an initial assessment is to see if the summary card has been completed:

	Age group (1990)					
	0–4 (n = 35)	5–14 (n = 80)	15–64 (n = 184)	65+ (n = 40)	Total (n = 345)	%
No. completed	31	75	152	38	286	83
No. blank	3	5	31	17	56	16
No. absent	1	1	1	1	3	1

There were no significant difference between males and females. In 1989 there were 39 (14%) blank cards and 13 (5%) absent summary cards.

Discussion

The completion of the card is the responsibility of the attending clinician. It allows better shared care and is an important source of epidemiological data. Although we are completing most, we must try to achieve 100% completion rates.

(C) PEFR measurements

We examined whether a PF recording had ever been taken for each patient. Of those taken during 1990, we looked at whether at least one of the last three recordings was within 80% of that predicted for each patient. We excluded the under fives.

Results: there were no significant differences between males and females.

	% of each age group			
PEFR ever recorded	5–14 (n = 80)	15–64 (n = 184)	65+ (n = 40)	Total (n = 310)
Yes	98	93	98	95
No	2	7	2	5

In 1989—92% were Yes and 8% were No

Good!

Nineteen patients were not seen in 1990, and did not need to be. They are excluded from the rest of the analysis in this section.

	% of each age group			
	5–14 (n = 78)	15–64 (n = 169)	65+ (n = 45)	Total (n = 295)
One of last PF recordings made in 1990 > 80% predicted	90	86	87	87
No PF recorded in 1990	10	14	13	13

All patients whose PF was recorded in 1990 had at least one reading greater than 80% predicted. In 1989 93% had a peak flow >80% predicted and only 4% had not had a recording.

Good! However we should try to use peak flow meters even more—they are the best and easiest objective assessment we have.

(D) Maintenance treatment?

How easy is it to identify the patient's maintenance treatment?

Maintenance treatment can be easily identified from the:	% of each age group				
	0–4 (n = 35)	5–14 (n = 80)	15–64 (n = 184)	65+ (n = 46)	Total (n = 345)
Summary card	49	26	20	33	26
Repeat prescription	34	30	33	44	34
Text	9	40	41	22	35
Total	91	96	94	99	95
Cannot be identified easily	9	4	6	1	5

Good, but could do better! For safe, effective shared care we all need to know what treatment the patient has been prescribed (and, we hope, using!).

(E) What mainten-ance treatments are being prescribed?

The 1989 audit established that 18% of all asthmatics were using bronchodilators only. This figure fell to 16% when children under the age of five were excluded. The BTS guidelines strongly recommend that all patients receive prophylactic therapy unless their asthma is very mild.

In this audit we looked at patients aged five or over taking bronchodilators only and who had needed more than two repeat prescriptions during the year.

Results

Bronchodilator	% of each age group			
	5–14 (n = 80)	15–64 (n = 184)	65+ (n = 46)	Total (n = 345)
Short-acting beta-agonist only	10	8	0	6.4
Theophyllines only	0	1*	0	0.3
Salmeterol only	0	0	0	0

*This patient was intolerant of inhaled steroids.

I think these data are a sign of the good asthma management we practise. Nevertheless four patients were identified as *excess* bronchodilator users and were promptly recalled for reassessment.

By implication 93% of all our asthmatics aged five or over were using either inhaled steroids or cromoglycate/nedocromil as prophylaxis, or solely required infrequent bronchodilator use. This compares favourably with other studies where this figure was 40–65% [3, 10, 11].

(F) Patients not seen in 1990

Nineteen patients on the asthma register were not seen in 1990 (5.5%), seventeen had received no treatment for asthma, none of whom had consulted for any respiratory tract complaints, and all of whom had previously had very mild asthma or there was some diagnostic doubt. It can be concluded that either they no longer had asthma, had never had it or that it was chronically quiescent. Should we remove them from the register?

One patient had had five repeat prescriptions for his inhaled salbutamol but had escaped all attempts at being seen. One patient firmly declines to receive asthma care from the practice, preferring to see a homeopathic veterinary surgeon. He requires occasional bronchodilators which we reluctantly prescribe. Thus over 99% of all our active asthmatics had been seen and assessed during the year. This was one of my original aims and we are obviously meeting it. Excellent.

(G) Hospital admissions due to asthma in 1990

Three males and two females were admitted, aged 1 to 64. All were admitted by the GPs. All were on full prophylactic treatment, *including* oral steroids. All had had their PF monitored prior to admission. All were nevertheless clinically deteriorating. In each case, appropriate care had been given prior to admission and each admission was fully justified. All five patients have severe asthma.

(H) Oral steroid courses

Traditionally oral steroids were used as a measure of last resort but increasingly we are recognizing that they are a useful part of our pharmacological armamentarium. We use them increasingly to diagnose asthma (by proving the obstruction to airflow can be reversed) and much more readily as part of *rescue* treatments. Accordingly it is not justifiable to assume that oral steroid use is a measure of treatment failure [4]. However, frequent use of oral steroids in patients not using preventers is probably a measure of poor care. We looked at the number of *courses* of steroids prescribed per patient in each age group, and at the preventer use in these patients aged over five.

Number of courses of oral steroids	% of each age group using oral steroids			
	5–14 (n = 80)	15–64 (n = 184)	65+ (n = 46)	Total (n = 310)
1	4	13	15	11
2	2	2	4	3
3	0	1	4	2
6	1	0	0	0.3
None	93	84	77	84.7

One patient is on continuous oral steroids, two patients each required a single course of oral steroids when not using inhaled steroids—both had very intermittent asthma which was severe when an attack occurred.

(J) Nebulizer use

We have recorded 13 patients who required nebulizations in 1990. We know of five patients who have home nebulizers (there may be some Canadians and Australians who have brought them to the UK about which we know nothing).

Of the five patients known to have home nebulizers, two are infants. The other three all have oral steroids at home and PF meters with self-management cards and all know how and when to escalate treatment and call for help. Eight patients thus required nebulizations from a doctor or nurse, of whom three received nebulizations at the initial presentation.

Of the remaining five patients, all have unstable asthma despite full doses of inhaled steroids. All are symptom-free most of the time.

Nebulization probably *is* a measure of outcome of the standard of asthma care. Particular care must be given after nebulization (see below). We are correctly not using nebulizers as an alternative to good preventative care. Some '*brittle*' asthmatics may always require occasional nebulizations.

Summary

The prevalence of diagnosed asthma in our practice is about average, although increasing especially in the older age groups. We have probably now identified nearly all the asthmatics in the practice so any further rises may well be due to an increased incidence. We are monitoring and managing our asthmatics very well, on the whole, but we need to maintain and even improve our high standards. We may not be recording all that we should, e.g. nebulizer use, oral steroid courses. We definitely should improve our peak flow recordings and the recording of each patient's current maintenance treatment.

Recommendations

1 That we make no changes now, but delay the next audit until January 1993 (i.e. auditing the year 1992). Then we can monitor the results of future changes more easily by having a year-end audit.
2 *Process 1*: we aim to record an expected and actual PF reading on all asthmatics at least annually. We also encourage PF ownership and self-management plans, and record these facts on the summary cards.
3 *Process 2*: we complete a summary card and update it for every patient.
4 *Process 3*: we continue to emphasize preventative drug use, and to record current maintenance treatment on the back of the summary card.
5 *Outcome 1*: we will follow protocols for nebulizer use and ongoing care. These protocols to be placed with each nebulizer.
6 *Outcome 2*: we continue to look critically at all asthma admissions and deaths.

Summary

Audit is an essential part of providing care to asthmatics in general practice. Audit should initially be simple and accentuate the positive, but as the practice experience and confidence grows, should be more complex and concentrate on highlighting the areas where improvements may be needed. Audit need not be time-consuming and can be interesting and a stimulant to raising standards and providing excellence. One of the most important concepts is to realize the importance of recording relevant, concise, objective data.

SUMMARY

Asthma is a complex disease. Despite much being known of its patho-genesis, and having excellent drugs with which to treat it, no cure is currently feasible. It is still a common cause of illness and sometimes death.

By applying and combining all that is known about successful asthma management, general practices should be able to provide good standards of care for asthmatics. This should lead to decreased morbidity and mortality, which in turn will lead to the greater satis-faction and happiness of asthmatics. The provision of such care should be by practice teams who should aim to work in partnership with asthmatics to improve their care.

SOURCES OF HELP

Asthma Management Centre: 232 Tower Street, Brunswick Business Park, Liverpool L3 4BJ.

Asthma Training Centre: Winton House, Church Road, Stratford Upon Avon, Warwickshire.

British Lung Foundation: 8 Peterborough Mews, London SW6 3BL.

British Society of Allergy and Immunology: Level D, South Academic Block, Southampton General Hospital, Tremona Road, Southampton.

British Thoracic Society: 1 Andrew's Place, London NW1 4LB.

General Practitioners in Asthma Group: The Medical Marketing Interface, Bath Brewery, Toll Bridge Road, Bath, BA1 7DE. They also produce a journal *Asthma in General Practice.*

National Asthma Campaign: Providence House, Providence Place, London N1 0NT.

Royal College of General Practitioners: 7, Prince's Gate, London SW7.

Allen and Hanburys Ltd: Stockley Park West, Uxbridge, Middlesex UB11 1BT.

Astra Pharmaceuticals Ltd: Home Park Estate, King's Langley, Hertfordshire WD4 8DU.

Boehringer Ingleheim Ltd: Southern Industrial Estate, Bracknell, Berkshire RG12 8YS.

Fisons Pharmaceuticals Ltd: Coleorton Hall, Coleorton, Leicestershire LE6 4GP.

Napp Laboratories Ltd: Cambridge Science Park, Milton Road, Cambridge CB4 4GW.

3M Health Care Ltd: Morley Street, Loughborough, Leicestershire LE11 1EP.

FURTHER READING

ABC of Asthma by J Rees and J Price. BMJ Publications, London

Asthma at Your Fingertips by M Levy, S Hilton and G Barnes. Class Publishing, London. A book for patients.

Asthma Management in Primary Care by R Pearson. Radcliffe Medical Press, Oxford.

Asthma–Who Cares? A manual for parents. Asthma Training Centre, Stratford upon Avon.

Asthma—Who Cares? A manual for teachers. Asthma Training Centre, Stratford upon Avon.

Asthma in Practice by M Levy and S Hilton. RCGP, London.

Essential Allergy by N Mygind. Blackwell Scientific Publications, Oxford.

Practical Management of Asthma by T Clarke and J Rees. Martin Dunitz, London.

REFERENCES

1. Introduction

1 British Thoracic Society *et al.* Guidelines on the management of asthma. *Thorax* 1993; **48**: 51–524 (suppl.).
2 Jones K. Asthma care in general practice—time for revolution? *Br J Gen Pract* 1991; **41**: 224–226.
3 Hilton S, Sibbald B, Anderson HP, Freeling P. Controlled evaluation of the effects of patient education on asthma morbidity in general practice. *Lancet* 1986; **i**: 26–29.
4 Stillwell B, Greenfield S, Drury M, Hull F. A nurse practitioner in general practice: working style and patterns of consultations. *J R Coll Gen Pract* 1987; **37**: 154–157.

2.1 Asthma—the disease

1 Teeling-Smith G. *Asthma.* Office of Health Economics, London, 1990 pp 4–6.
2 International Asthma Management Project. International Consensus Report on the Diagnosis and Management of Asthma. *Clin Exp Allergy* 1992; **22**: 1 (supp. 1).
3 Anderson HR. Is the prevalence of asthma changing? *Arch Dis Child* 1989; **64**: 172–175.
4 Jones K. Asthma—still a challenge for general practice. *J R Coll Gen Pract* 1989; **39**: 254–256.
5 Clifford RD, Radford M, Howell JB *et al.* Prevalence of respiratory symptoms among seven and eleven year old school children and association with asthma. *Arch Dis Child* 1989; **64**: 1118–1125.
6 Burr MI, Butland BK, King J *et al.* Changes in asthma prevalence: two surveys 15 years apart. *Arch Dis Child* 1989; **64**: 1452–1456.
7 Khan TK, Russell G. Respiratory symptoms and atopy in Aberdeen school children: evidence from two surveys 25 years apart. *B M J* 1992; **304**: 873–875.
8 Burney PGJ, Chinn S, Rona RJ. Has the prevalence of asthma increased in children? Evidence from the national study of health and growth 1973–1986. *B M J* 1990; **300**: 1306–1310.
9 Matagy AK, Howell JRB, Waters WE. Respiratory symptoms and bronchial reactivity: identification of a syndrome and its relation to asthma. *B M J* 1986; **293**: 525–529.
10 Gellert AR, Gellert SL, Iliffe SR. Prevalence and management of asthma in a London inner city general practice. *Br J Gen Pract* 1990; **40**: 197–201.
11 Fitzgerald JM, Sears MR, Roberts RS, Morris MM, Fester GA, Hargreave FE. School absenteeism due to under-diagnosis and under treatment of asthma in Canadian school children. *Clin Invest Med* 1988; **II**: R-665, c105.
12 Robertson CF, Heycock E, Bishop J, Nolan T, Olinsky A, Phelan ID. Prevalence of asthma in Melbourne school children: changes over 26 years. *B M J* 1991; **302**: 1116–1118.
13 Barry DMJ, Burr ML, Limb ES. Prevalence of asthma among 12 year old school children in New Zealand and South Wales: a comparative survey. *Thorax* 1991; **46**: 405–409.
14 Fry J, Sandler G, Brooks D. *Disease Data Book*, MTP Press Ltd, Lancaster, 1989; 72.
15 Spark R, Holgate ST, Platts-Mills TAE, Cogswell JJ. Exposure to house dust mite allergen and the development of asthma in childhood: a prospective study. *N Engl J Med* 1990; **323**: 502–507.
16 International Workshop on Mite Allergens and Asthma. *J Allergy Clin Immunol* 1989; **83**: 416.

17 Godfrey K. House dust mite avoidance: the way forward. *Clin Exp Allergy* 1991; **21**: 1–2.

18 International Asthma Management Project. International Consensus Report on the Diagnosis and Management of Asthma. *Clin Exp Allergy* 1992; **22-1**: 3–4.

19 Scadding JG. Definition and Clinical Categories of Asthma. In: Clark T and Godfrey S eds. *Asthma* 2nd edn. Chapman and Hall, London, 1983; 1–10.

20 Jenkins RM. An audit and strategy for asthma in general practice. *Mod Med* 1988; **33**: 888–897.

21 Rona RJ, Guilliford MC, Chinn S. Effects of prematurity and intra-uterine growth on respiratory health and lung function in childhood. *B M J* 1993; **306**: 817–820.

22 Ramsdale EH, Morris MM, Roberts RS, Hargreave FE. Asymptomatic bronchial hyper-responsiveness in rhinitis. *J Allergy Clin Immunol* 1985; **75**: 573–577.

23 Slavin RG, Cannon RF, Friedman WH, Palitang E, Sundaram M. Sinusitis and bronchial asthma. *J Allergy Clin Immunol* 1980; **66**: 250–257.

24 Anonymous. *National Asthma Survey Results.* Action Asthma, Allen and Hanbury's Ltd. Uxbridge, 1991; 5–13.

25 Turner-Warwick M. Nocturnal asthma: a study in general practice. *J R Coll Gen Pract* 1989; **39**: 239–243.

26 Anonymous. *The Life Quality of Asthmatics.* Applied Research and Communications Ltd, London, 1990; 6–7, 10–15, 19.

27 Burney PGJ. Asthma mortality in England and Wales—evidence for a further increase, 1974–84. *Lancet* 1986; **ii**: 323–326.

28 Berrill WT. Is the death rate from asthma exaggerated? Evidence from West Cumbria. *B M J* 1993; **306**: 193–194.

29 Judd M, Jolly K. Death rate from asthma. *B M J* 1993; **306**: 518.

30 Clark TJH. *The Occurrence and Cost of Asthma.* Cambridge Medical Publications Ltd, Worthing, 1990; 4–7, 10–13, 20–23.

31 Reid JJ. The early diagnosis and possible primary prevention of asthma. *Proceedings of 13th WONCA Conference, Vancouver, Canada, May 9–14 1992.*

32 Peak JK, Woolcock AJ, Cullen K. Rate of decline of lung function in subjects with asthma. *Eur J Respir Dis* 1987; **70**: 171–179.

33 Van Shayck CP, Dompeling E, Folgering H, Verbeck ACM, van den Hoogen H, van Herwaarden CLA, van Weel C. Effects of continuous versus symptomatic bronchodilator treatment during two years in asthma and COPD. *Proceedings of the 13th WONCA Conference, Vancouver, Canada, May 9–14 1992.*

34 McCarthy TP. Nebulised budesonide in severe childhood asthma. *Lancet* 1989; **i**: 379–380.

35 Kerrebijn ICF, Van Ess-Zandrhet EM, Neijens HJ. Effect of long-term treatment with inhaled corticosteroids and beta agonists on the bronchial responsiveness in children with asthma. *J Allergy Clin Immunol* 1987; **79**: 653–659.

36 Horn CR, Clark TJH, Cochrane GM. Can the morbidity of asthma be reduced by high dose inhaled therapy? A prospective trial. *Thorax* 1988; **43**: 252.

2.2 Asthma—management

1 Teeling-Smith G. *Asthma.* Office of Health Economics, London, 1990; 4.

2 Hilton S. Patient education in asthma. *Fam Pract* 1986; **3**: 44–48.

3 Hilton S, Sibbald B, Anderson HR, Freeling P. Controlled education of the effects of patient education on asthma morbidity in general practice. *Lancet* 1986; **i**: 26–29.

4 Beasley R, Cushley M, Holgate ST. A self-management plan in the treatment of adult asthma. *Thorax* 1989; **44**: 200–204.

5 British Thoracic Society *et al.* Guidelines for the management of asthma in adults: I—chronic persistent asthma. *B M J* 1990; **301**: 651–653.

6 British Thoracic Society *et al.* Guidelines for the management of asthma in adults: II—acute severe asthma. *B M J* 1990; **301**: 797–800.

7 Godfrey K. House dust mite avoidance: the way forward. *J Clin Exp Allergy* 1991; **21**: 1–2.

8 Wall M, Bocks J, Holsclaw D, Reeding G. Health effects of smoking on children. *Am Rev Respir Dis* 1985; **132**: 1137–1138.

9 Kjelmann NIM. Effect of parental smoking on IgE levels in children. *Lancet* 1989; **i**: 993–994.

10 Brunette MG, Lands L, Thibodau L-P. Childhood asthma: prevention of attacks with short term corticosteroid treatment of upper respiratory tract infections. *Paediatrics* 1988; **81**: 624–626.

11 Rees J. Beta agonists and asthma. *B M J* 1991; **302**: 1166–1167.

12 Van Schayck CP, Dompeling E, van Herwaarden CLA. Bronchodilator treatment in moderate asthma or chronic bronchitis: continuous or on demand? A randomised controlled study. *B M J* 1991; **303**: 1426–1431.

13 Fitzpatrick MF, Mackay T, Driver T, Douglas NJ. Salmeterol in nocturnal asthma: a double blind placebo controlled trial of a long acting Beta 2 agonist. *B M J* 1990; **301**: 1365–1368.

14 Cheung D, Timmers C, Zwinderman AH *et al.* Long term effects of a long-acting B2 adrenoceptor agonist, salmeterol, on airway hyper-responsiveness in patients with mild asthma. *N Engl J Med* 1992; **327**: 1198–1203.

15 O'Driscoll BR, Taylor RJ, Horsy MG, Chambers DK, Bernstein A. Nebulized salbutamol with and without ipratropium bromide in acute airflow obstruction. *Lancet* 1989; **i**: 1418–1420.

16 Horn CR, Clark TJH, Cochrane GM. Can the morbidity of asthma be reduced by high dose inhaled therapy? A prospective trial. *Thorax* 1988; **43**: 252.

17 Reed CE. Aerosol steroids as primary treatment of mild asthma. *New Eng J Med* 1991; **325**: 425–426.

18 Brown PH, Blundell G, Greering AP, Crompton GK. Do large volume spacer devices reduce the systemic effects of high dose inhaled corticosteroids? *Thorax* 1990; **45**: 736–739.

19 Balfour-Lynn L. Growth and childhood asthma. *Arch Dis Child* 1986; **61**: 1049–1055.

20 Shohat M, Shohat T, Kedem R, Mimouri M, Danon YL. Childhood asthma and growth outcome. *Arch Dis Child* 1987; **62**: 63–65.

21 Phillips GH. Structure-activity relationships of topically active steroids: the selection of fluticasone proprionate. *Respir Med* 1990; **84** (suppl. A): 19–23.

22 Harding SM. Human pharmacology of fluticasone proprionate. *Proceedings of the European Academy of Allergologie and Clinical Immunology* 1989; Berlin West, Symposia Review: 15–17.

23 Silk H, Guay-Woodford L, Perez-Atayde R, Geha RS, Broff M. Fatal varicella in steroid dependent asthma. *J Allergy Clin Immunol* 1988; **81**: 47–51.

24 Eigen H, Reid JJ, Daln R, Del Bufalo C, Fasano L, Gunelle G *et al.* Evaluation of the addition of cromolyn sodium to bronchodilator maintenance therapy in the long term management of asthma. *J Allergy Clin Immun* 1987; **80**: 612–621.

25 Newman SP, Millar AB, Lennard-Jones TR, Moren F, Clarke SW. Improvements of pressurised aerosol deposition with Nebuhaler spacer device. *Thorax* 1984; **34**: 935–941.

26 McCarthy TP. Rapid response to budesonide inhaled in a Nebuhaler in asthmatic children. *Br J Clin Pract* 1990; **44**: 180-182.

27 British Thoracic Sociey *et al.* Guidelines on the management of asthma. *Thorax* 1993; **48**: S7 (suppl.).

28 O'Callaghan C, Milner AO, Swarbrick A. Spacer device with face mask attachment for giving bronchodilators to infants with asthma. *B M J* 1989; **298**: 160–161.

29 Warner JD, Niejens HJ *et al.* Asthma: a follow up statement from an international paediatric asthma consensus group. *Arch Dis Child* 1992; **67**: 240-248.

30 Charlton I, Charlton G, Broomfield J, Mullee M. Evaluation of peak flow and symptoms only self management plans for control of asthma in general practice. *B M J* 1990; **301**: 1355-1359.

31 International Asthma Management Project. International Consensus Report on the Diagnosis and Management of Asthma. *Clin Exp Allergy* 1992; **22**: suppl. 1, 1–72.

32 Slavin RG, Cannon RF, Friedman WH, Palitang E, Sundaram M. Sinusitis and bronchial asthma. *J Allergy Clin Immunol.* 1980; **66**: 250–257.

33 Shatz M, Harden KM, Forsythe A *et al.* The course of asthma during pregnancy, post partum and with successive pregnancies: a prospective analysis. *J Allergy Clin Immunol* 1988; **81**: 509.

34 Management of Asthma During Pregnancy. *Report of the Working Party on Asthma and Pregnancy.* NIH Publications No. 93-3279A, 1993.

35 Slepian IK, Mathews KP, McLean JA. Aspirin sensitive asthma. *Chest* 1985; **87**: 386–391.

36 Cookson WO, Sharp PA, Faux JA, Hopkins JM. Linkage between IgE responses underlying asthma and rhinitis and chromosome II. *Lancet* 1989; **i**: 1292–1295.

37 Busse WW. Respiratory infections: their role in airway responsiveness and the pathogenesis of asthma. *J Allergy Clin Immunol* 1990; **85**: 671–688.

38 Sibbald B, White P, Pharoah C. Relationship between psychosocial factors an asthma morbidity. *Fam Pract* 1988; **5**: 12–17.

39 Struck RC. Identification of the fatality-prone subjects with asthma. *J Allergy Clin Immunol* 1989; **83**: 477–485.

40 Anonymous. *The Reporting of Injuries, Diseases and Dangerous Occurrences Regulations 1985.* Health and Safety Executive, London, 4–5.

41 *British National Formulary.* Sections 3.1–3.3 March 1993.

42 *Monthly Index of Medical Specialities.* Section 11a. April 1993.

3 The asthma clinic

1 British Thoracic Society *et al.* Guideline on the management of asthma. *Thorax* 93; **48**: S2 (suppl.).

2 International Asthma Management Project. International Consensus Report on the Diagnosis and Management of Asthma. *Clin Exp Allergy* 1992; **22**: suppl. 1, 1–2.

3 Charlton I, Charlton G, Broomfield J, Mullee M. Evaluation of peak flow and symptom only self-management plans for control of asthma in general practice. *B M J* 1990; **301**: 1355–1359.

4 Audit

1 Anonymous. *Action Asthma: Asthma Audit Protocol.* Allen and Hanbury's Ltd, Uxbridge, 1992, 2–7.

2 Barritt PW, Davies R. Measuring success in asthma care. *Fam Pract* 1986; **3**: 229–234.

3 Gellert AR, Gellert SL, Iliffe SR. Prevalence and treatment of asthma in a London inner city practice. *Br J Gen Pract* 1990; **40**: 199–201.

4 Barritt PW, Staples EB. Measuring success in asthma care: a repeat audit. *Br J Gen Pract* 1991; **41**: 232–236.

5 McCarthy TP, Taylor MD, Richardson PDI. The management of asthma using clinical protocols: is it cost effective and does it improve patients' lifestyles? *Br J Med Econ* 1992; **2**: 13–24.

6 Charlton I, Charlton G, Broomfield G, Mullee M. Audit of the effect of a nurse run asthma clinic on workload and patients morbidity in a general practice. *Br J Gen Pract* 1991; **41**: 227–231.

7 Hilton S, Sibbald S, Anderson HR, Freeling P. Controlled evaluation of the effects of patients education on asthma morbidity in general practice. *Lancet* 1986; **i**: 26–29.

8 Jenkins RM. An audit and strategy for asthma in general practice. *Mod Med* 1988; **33**: 888–897.

9 Crockett AWB. Audit of provision of asthma care in a small rural practice in the UK. *Proceedings of the 13th WONCA Conference, Vancouver, Canada May 9–14 1992.*

10 Turner-Warwick M. Nocturnal asthma: a study in general practice. *J R Coll Gen Pract* 1989; **39:** 239–243.

11 Horn CR, Cochrane GM. Management of asthma in general practice. *Respir Med* 1989; **83:** 67–70.

INDEX